W. H. AUDEN

*The Sea and
the Mirror*

W. H. AUDEN: CRITICAL EDITIONS

GENERAL EDITOR
Edward Mendelson

Lectures on Shakespeare
Reconstructed and edited by
Arthur Kirsch

Juvenilia: Poems, 1922–1928
Expanded Paperback Edition
Edited by Katherine Bucknell

The Sea and the Mirror
A Commentary on Shakespeare's The Tempest
Edited by Arthur Kirsch

W. H. AUDEN

The Sea and
the Mirror

* * *

A Commentary on
Shakespeare's *The Tempest*

EDITED BY

Arthur Kirsch

PRINCETON UNIVERSITY PRESS
PRINCETON AND OXFORD

Published by Princeton University Press, 41 William Street,
Princeton, New Jersey 08540
In the United Kingdom: Princeton University Press, 6 Oxford Street,
Woodstock, Oxfordshire OX20 1TW

Third printing, and first paperback printing, 2005
Paperback ISBN: 978-0-691-12384-4

The Library of Congress has cataloged the cloth edition of this book as follows
Auden, W. H. (Wystan Hugh), 1907–1973.
The sea and the mirror : a commentary on Shakespeare's
The tempest / W. H. Auden ; edited by Arthur Kirsch.
p.   cm. — (W. H. Auden—critical editions)
Includes bibliographical references.
ISBN 0-691-11371-8 (acid-free paper)
1. Survival after airplane accidents, shipwrecks, etc.–Poetry.
2. Fathers and daughters–Poetry.   3. Castaways–
Poetry.   4. Magicians–Poetry.   5. Islands–Poetry.
6. Shakespeare, William, 1564–1616. Tempest.
I. Shakespeare, William, 1564–1616. Tempest.
II. Kirsch, Arthur C.   III. Title.   IV. Series.
PR2878.T4 A84   2003
811'.52–dc21   2002030262

British Library Cataloging-in-Publication Data is available

This book has been composed in New Baskerville
Designed by Jan Lilly
Composed by Eileen Reilly

Printed on acid-free paper. ∞

press.princeton.edu

Printed in the United States of America

5   7   9   10   8   6

CONTENTS

PREFACE

"The Sea and the Mirror: A Commentary on Shakespeare's *The Tempest*" was perhaps the only one of his works that Auden ventured to describe (in a letter to a friend) as "important." It was the most brilliant and ambitious in a series of long poems he wrote after emigrating to the United States in 1939 and returning to the Anglican Communion in 1940. The poem was written from 1942 to 1944, in the midst of World War II, and published in 1944 together with another long poem, "For the Time Being: A Christmas Oratorio," in a volume entitled *For the Time Being*. Auden told friends that "The Sea and the Mirror" was "really about the Christian conception of art," and it stands as his most profound exploration of the Christian aesthetic that underlies much of his poetic canon.

Auden also wrote, in another letter to a friend, that "The Sea and the Mirror" is "my Ars Poetica, in the same way I believe *The Tempest* to be Shakespeare's," and the poem's relation to its Shakespearean original is at the heart of much of its fascination and depth. Auden was preoccupied with Shakespeare throughout the 1940s, and this edition points to many connections between the poem and the year-long series of lectures he delivered in 1946–47 at the New School for Social Research as well as the later criticism of Shakespeare he published in *The Dyer's Hand*. "The Sea and the Mirror" ranks as a great poem in itself, but it also offers one of the twentieth century's most profound interpretations of Shakespeare's play. The dramatic action of Auden's poem takes place in a theater after the curtain has come down on a performance of *The Tempest*. It includes a moving, elegiac speech in which Prospero bids farewell to Ariel, then a sequence of dazzling metrical and linguistic virtuosity in which the remaining characters respond to their experiences on the island; and ends with an extravagantly inventive speech in which the uncivilized Caliban delivers a disquisition on art in a prose style based on the later manner of Henry James. Auden was especially proud of Caliban's speech, which he frequently reprinted in selections of his poetry, and it is an unalloyed example of what his friend the neurologist and writer Oliver Sacks has called his "wild, extraordinary and demonic imagination."

The edition incorporates for the first time corrections that Auden made on the Random House galleys of the first edition of the poem in 1944 and that the proofreaders or compositor ignored. The notes to this edition also quote from the notebooks in which Auden drafted the poem, one of them in the Poetry Collection of the State University of New York at Buffalo, the other in the Henry W. and Albert A. Berg Collection of English and American Literature at the New York Public Library. Both notebooks, together with Auden's proof corrections, have made it possible to trace almost the whole genesis of the poem, and to observe Auden at work, playing with words, experimenting with rhymes and stanzas, altering and refining his meanings, and creating perhaps the greatest work of his career.

MY MOST substantial debt is to the knowledge, skill, and encouragement of Edward Mendelson, Auden's literary executor and general editor. He read every word of this edition, in manuscript as well as proof, occasionally helped me decipher Auden's often maddeningly difficult handwriting, led me to many relevant sources, and corrected many mistakes. I also drew deeply upon his extensive published work on Auden, including *Early Auden* (New York: Viking Press, 1981) and *Later Auden* (New York: Farrar, Straus and Giroux, 1999) as well as his editions of Auden's poetry, prose, and libretti. This edition would not have been possible without his work. I am also greatly indebted to John Fuller's richly informative *W. H. Auden: A Commentary* (London: Faber and Faber, 1998; Princeton: Princeton University Press, 1998).

I owe a more general debt to the larger community of Auden scholars. Several specific points in the notes to this edition were suggested by Alan Ansen's unpublished essay on "The Sea and the Mirror" that is held by the Berg Collection of the New York Public Library. Ansen wrote the essay while he was a student in Auden's course on Shakespeare at the New School in 1946–47. He subsequently became Auden's secretary and friend.

I had quite extraordinarily generous assistance from Robert Bertholf, Curator of Poetry and Rare Books at the University of Buffalo. I am also grateful for the considerable amount of time spent on my behalf by Stephen Crook and Philip Milito at the Berg Collection of the New York Public Library. Heather Moore, at the Alderman Library of the University of Virginia, has been continuously gracious and helpful. I owe much to the great skill, wisdom, and kindness of Lauren Lepow as well as of Mary Murrell, Jan Lilly, and Eileen Reilly at Princeton University Press.

I am, finally, thankful to my wife Beverly for her knowledge of editing as well as her love and her unfailing sense of proportion about problems I encountered in completing the book.

INTRODUCTION

The Poem

"The Sea and the Mirror" represents a diversity of Auden's intellectual and emotional interests, but as its subtitle indicates, it is first of all "A Commentary on Shakespeare's *The Tempest*." Auden was drawn to *The Tempest* for many reasons. As he told a lecture audience in his course on Shakespeare at the New School for Social Research in 1947, *The Tempest* is a mythopoeic work, an example of a genre that encourages adaptations, including his own, inspiring "people to go on for themselves . . . to make up episodes that [the author] as it were, forgot to tell us." Auden also, like many critics before and since, understood *The Tempest* as a skeptical work. When he wrote that "The Sea and the Mirror" was his Art of Poetry, "in the same way" he believed *The Tempest* to be Shakespeare's, he added, "ie I am attempting something which in a way is absurd, to show in a work of art, the limitations of art." In the concluding lecture of his course at the New School, Auden especially praised Shakespeare for his consciousness of these limitations: "There's something a little irritating in the determination of the very greatest artists, like Dante, Joyce, Milton, to create masterpieces and to think themselves important. To be able to devote one's life to art without forgetting that art is frivolous is a tremendous achievement of personal character. Shakespeare never takes himself too seriously." Neither did Auden, and "The Sea and the Mirror," which he wrote in the shadow of war, is a testament to his own artistic humility.

The central limit of art that Shakespeare deals with in *The Tempest*, and that Auden explores in "The Sea and the Mirror," is that art is doubly illusory, because it holds the mirror up to nature rather than to the truth that passes human understanding. In *The Tempest*, a play that from first to last presents itself as an illusion of an illusion, Prospero renounces his art, and in the Epilogue his renunciation is associated with the spiritual reality represented in the Lord's Prayer:

> Now I want
> Spirits to enforce, art to enchant;
> And my ending is despair
> Unless I be reliev'd by prayer,
> Which pierces so that it assaults
> Mercy itself and frees all faults.
> As you from crimes would pardon'd be,
> Let your indulgence set me free.

After Auden's return in 1940 to the Anglican Church, a spiritual renewal that was intensified in August 1941 by the death of his mother, with whom his faith was deeply intertwined, he immersed himself in the writings of Kierkegaard and other existential religious philosophers, as well as of Saint Augustine and Pascal, and became preoccupied with theological issues. In November 1942 he wrote in the Roman Catholic journal *Commonweal*, "As a writer, who is also a would-be Christian, I cannot help feeling that a satisfactory theory of Art from the standpoint of the Christian faith has yet to be worked out." "The Sea and the Mirror" constitutes Auden's attempt, with the example of Shakespeare, to work out that theory.

The Tempest's exploration of the idea of art is enacted within a dualistic, allegorical structure, with Prospero as well as most of the rest of the cast poised between the animalistic representation of Caliban and the nonhuman figure of Ariel, the former variously interpreted by critics as nature, the flesh, the id, the latter as the immaterial, the spirit, imagination. Auden's interest in Augustine made him especially susceptible to this opposition in the play. He wrote to Stephen Spender in 1942, "I have been reading St Augustine a lot lately who is quite wonderful," and he took notes on *The Confessions* at the end of the notebook in which he drafted "For the Time Being" and parts of "The Sea and the Mirror." *The Confessions* is reflected not only in a number of important details in "The Sea and the Mirror," particularly in Prospero's speech, but also in Auden's broader identification in the poem with Augustine's rejection of the temptations of Manichaeism, as well as of rhetoric. In a 1954 essay on *The Tempest*, Auden wrote:

> As a biological organism Man is a natural creature subject to the necessities of nature; as a being with consciousness and will, he is at the same time a historical person with the freedom of the spirit. *The Tempest* seems to me a manichean work, not because it shows the relation of Nature to Spirit as one of conflict and hostility, which in fallen man it is, but because it puts the blame for this upon Nature and makes the Spirit innocent.

He added, "It is unfortunate that the word 'Flesh,' set in contrast to 'Spirit,' is bound to suggest not what the Gospels and St. Paul intended it to mean, the whole physical-historical nature of fallen man, but his physical nature alone, a suggestion very welcome to our passion for reproving and improving others instead of examining our own consciences."

Though Auden objected to what he considered Shakespeare's Manichaean opposition of Ariel and Caliban and its spiritual elevation of Prospero's art, the schematic dualism itself was nonetheless potent to him and was perhaps the fundamental reason why he chose to adapt *The Tempest*. Caliban is in constant counterpoint with Ariel in *The Tempest*—they cannot exist without each other—and their opposition informs or reflects everything else in the play. Antonio and Sebastian's unregenerate rapaciousness and desperation contrast throughout with Gonzalo's beneficence and hopefulness. Venus is counterpointed with Ceres within the wedding masque, and the conspiracy of Caliban, Stephano, and Trinculo complements as well as disrupts the performance of the masque, the high artifice and graciousness of which remain in our memory as much as the drunken malice of the conspiracy remains in Prospero's.

Similarly, Miranda's celebrated lines, "O brave new world / That has such people in't," coexist with Prospero's answer, " 'Tis new to thee" (5.1.183–84). Neither response takes precedence: innocence and experience, youth and age, are as consubstantial in the play as good and evil.

Auden was deeply preoccupied with dualism throughout his early career. *The Orators* (1932), for example, a long work in a mixture of prose and verse whose structure and themes he revisited in "The Sea and the Mirror," deals with the duality of the one and the many, with "Private faces in public places," with a wounded individual in conflict with himself as well as his society, with a homosexual poet's relation to his vocation and his audience. The poem attempts to find psychological and political ways of understanding these dualities, but with mixed success. "The Sea and the Mirror" places them in a theological context, refocusing and subsuming them in a Christian faith that can at once redeem an individual and constitute his community. But the dualities nonetheless remain, and Auden continued to be concerned with them at the time he composed "The Sea and the Mirror." In 1939 in his unfinished prose work *The Prolific and the Devourer,* as well as in *The Double Man* in 1941, he explored the "dualistic division between either The Whole and its parts, or one part of the whole and another" that characterizes "the false philosophy," and in both works he made distinctions that were essentially the same as those he later used in his criticism of the Manichaeism of *The Tempest.* Auden's hope of transcending such dualities informed his religious epistemology—"*credo ut intelligam,*" he said, quoting Saint Anselm, "I believe in order that I may understand"—but dualistic dichotomies nonetheless abided in his thought. In one of his introductions to his five-volume *Poets of the English Language* in 1950, he wrote that "the dualism inaugurated by Luther, Machiavelli and Descartes has brought us to the end of our tether and we know that either we must discover a unity which can repair the fissures that separate the individual from society, feeling from intellect, and conscience from both, or we shall surely die by spiritual despair and physical annihilation." In a celebrated line in "September 1, 1939," he had said more simply, but analogously, "We must love one another or die." While he was writing "The Sea and the Mirror," Auden composed and made available to a seminar he was teaching at Swarthmore an extraordinarily detailed and comprehensive chart of antitheses, in all aspects of human life and thought, defining the "Dualism of Experience" in "This World," the world that emerged after the Fall and the loss of Eden, and that only charity can redeem. Many of the oppositions and reconciliations of this synoptic chart are reflected in "The Sea and the Mirror." Several appear directly in Caliban's speech in Chapter III, and several more are the subject of Alonso's speech in Chapter II, which was probably composed at the same time as the chart.

There was also a personal focus and urgency for Auden in this kind of antithetical thinking. In April 1939, after his emigration to the United States, Auden met Chester Kallman, an American fourteen years his junior; he fell in love, a love he had sought, he said, since he was a child, and entered into a relationship with Kallman that he regarded as the moral equivalent of a marriage. In July 1941 Kallman revealed that he had betrayed him with another lover, and the effect on Auden was profound. On Christmas Day 1941, he wrote a passionate letter to Kallman, with an extraordinary mixture of erotic and religious imagery, celebrating the sacramental union he still hoped for:

> Because it is in you, a Jew, that I, a Gentile, inheriting an O-so-genteel anti-semitism, have found my happiness:
>
> As this morning I think of Bethlehem, I think of you.
>
> .   .   .   .
>
> Because, suffering on your account the torments of sexual jealousy, I have had a glimpse of the infinite vileness of masculine conceit;

PARADISE
(Eden)
Essential Being
The Fall

	HELL of the Pure Deed — Power without Purpose		THIS WORLD — Dualism of Experience / Knowledge of Good and Evil / Existential Being			HELL of the Pure Word — Knowledge without Power	
	← Search for Salvation by finding refuge in Nature				→ Search for Salvation by finding release from Nature		
Primary Symbol	Sea	Common Night	Forest	City	Mountain	Private Light	Desert
Secondary Symbols	Blood	Tears · Serpents	Wild Beasts	Domestic Pets	Birds	Machines · Insects	Abstract shapes
Myth Symbols	Dragons	Sirens · Hidden Treasure	Dwarves Giants	The Hero · The Ring	Witches	Ghosts	The Magician's Castle
Metaphysical Condition	Pure Aesthetic Immediacy	Pure Ethical Potentiality	Art	Actualization of the Possible · Growth · Soul=Spirit	Science	Aesthetic Nonentity	Pure Ethical Actuality
Order	Monist Unity (water)	Barbaric Vagueness	Rivers · Country	Differentiated Unity · Civilization	Roads · Town	Dissociated Multiplicity	Decadent Triviality
Time	Natural · Cyclical · Reversible	Everlasting Circle change ○	Historical	Irreversible · Spiral ℓℓℓℓ	Process Change	Static · Eternal · Unchanging	Turbine ◎
Relation between Selves	Mutual Irresponsibility Encroachment		The Vow	Conscious relations · Neighborliness	The Contract	Mutual Aversion Desertion	
Relation to Self	Self-sufficiency		Low brow Masses	Self-Realization	High brow Rulers	Self-negation	
Mental Life	Stream of Sensations		Sensation · Memory · Intuition	Generalized patterns of feeling · Important fact	Thinking · Logic · Feeling	Empty Abstractions	
Requiredness	Objective · Instinctive Determined		Venere Vulgare · Blind Eros	Subjective Grace · Agape	Venere Celeste · Seeing Anteros	Conscious lack of requiredness · The void Indecision or Self-Reflection	
Sin	Sensuality		Criminals	Anxiety	Police	Pride	
			Bohemians		Bourgeois Pharisees		
Sex	Incest (The Walsung)		Romantic Adultery (Tristan)	Marriage	Sophisticated Adultery (Figaro)	Promiscuity (Don Giovanni)	
Physical Diseases	Cancer		Digestive-Venereal		Sensory-Respiratory	Paralysis	
Mental Diseases	Idiocy		Epileptics Manic-Depressive		Paranoiacs Schizophrenics	Dementia Praecox	
Religion	Blind Superstition (Animism)		Pantheism	(Cath.) Faith (Prot.)	Deism	Lucid Cynicism (Logical Positivism)	
Theories			Irrational Emotionalism		Rational Legalism		
Art	Dada Art		Surrealism		Cubism	State Art	
Politics	Tyranny (Fascism)		Feudal Aristocracy		Laissez Faire Democracy	Anarchy (Economic Collapse Class War)	
Political Slogans	Fraternity			Justice		Liberty	
Hero	The Tragic Hero-Outlaw with S[ex] A[ppeal] / Flying Dutchman · Vamp		The Comic or Ironic Hero · Don Quixote · The Beggar · Byron's Don Juan · The Idiot (Dost.) · The Child (Alice) · Marx Bros.		Detectives (Holmes)	The Demonic Villain without natural S[ex] A[ppeal] · Iago · Stavrogin · The Grand Inquisitor · Depraved or Cissy Master-Crooks	
The Quest	The Voluntary Journey of the corrupt mind through the Sea. Purgation of pride by Dissolution		Fertilizing the Wasteland · PURGATORY · Draining the Swamp · The Island · Forgiveness · The Oasis			The Voluntary Journey of the corrupt body through the Desert. Purgation of Lust by Dessication	

PARADISE
(The City of God)

As this morning, I think of Joseph, I think of you.

Because mothers have much to do with your queerness and mine, because we have both lost ours, and because Mary is a camp name;
    As this morning I think of Mary, I think of you.

. . . .

Because, on account of you, I have been, in intention, and almost in act, a murderer;
    As this morning I think of Herod, I think of you.

. . . .

Because I believe in your creative gift, and because I rely absolutely upon your critical judgement,
    As this morning I think of the Magi, I think of you.

Because you alone know the full extent of my human weakness, and because I think I know yours, because of my resentment against being small and your resentment against having a spinal curvature, and because with my body I worship yours;
    As this morning I think of the Manhood, I think of you.

Because it is through you that God has chosen to show me my beatitude,
    As this morning I think of the Godhead, I think of you.

Because in the eyes of our bohemian friends our relationship is absurd;
    As this morning I think of the Paradox of the Incarnation,
    I think of you.

Because, although our love, beginning Hans Anderson, became Grimm, and there are probably even grimmer tests to come, nevertheless I believe that if only we have faith in God and in each other, we shall be permitted to realize all that love is intended to be;

As this morning I think of the Good Friday and the Easter
Sunday implicit in Christmas Day, I think of you.

This remarkable letter is an elegy, however, not an epithalamium.
Auden and Kallman remained intimate friends for the rest of their
lives and often lived together, but the relationship became more
that of parent and child. They were not again lovers, and Auden's
hope of achieving the mystical union of flesh and spirit he yearned
for remained unfulfilled.

Both the hope and disappointment were intensified for him by
his homosexuality. On 20 February 1943, in the midst of writing
"The Sea and the Mirror," Auden told Elizabeth Mayer, "Being 'an-
ders wie die Andern' [different from others] has its troubles. There
are days when the knowledge that there will never be a place which
I can call home, that there will never be a person with whom I shall
be one flesh, seems more than I can bear. . . ." Kallman's betrayal,
"The Crisis" in "l'affaire C," as Auden later called it, directly under-
lies Prospero's lyrics in Chapter I of "The Sea and the Mirror": "*In-
form my hot heart straight away / Its treasure loves another.*" But Auden's
relation to Kallman also affects the representation of Caliban and
Ariel in "The Sea and the Mirror," and indeed the whole conception
of art that Auden develops. In letters to Christopher Isherwood and
Theodore Spencer in 1944, he identified "Caliban (The Prick) as
the representative of Nature" and Ariel "as the representative of
Spirit," and to Isherwood he also remarked, "It's OK to say that Ariel
is Chester, but Chester is also Caliban, 'das lebendigste', ie Ariel is
Caliban seen in the mirror." *Das Lebendigste*, the one most loved, is
an allusion to the homosexual loved one in Hölderlin's "Sokrates
und Alkibiades," a poem to which Auden often referred and that
he quoted in full in his lecture on Shakespeare's *Sonnets* at the New
School. In 1939, in *The Prolific and the Devourer*, Auden wrote:

At first the baby sees his limbs as belonging to the outside
world. When he has learnt to control them, he accepts them as

parts of himself. What we call the "I," in fact, is the area over which our will is immediately operative. Thus, if we have a toothache, we seem to be two people, the suffering "I" and the hostile outer world of the tooth. His penis never fully belongs to a man.

Auden often repeated this statement and clearly meant it as a Pauline description of a division that exists in all men. Nevertheless, his own sense of division appears to have been emphatic, and his identification of Chester with the *lebendigste*, but ungovernably phallic, Caliban as well as with Ariel, who represented the Muse to Shakespeare as well as to him, also suggests that he saw an intersection between his vocation as a poet and his own sexual nature. The association between the two is made explicit in another letter to Isherwood in which Auden wrote that he expected critics "to jump on the James pastiche" he used to depict Caliban "and think it is unseemly frivolity. Art is like queerness. You may defend it or you may attack it. But people never forgive you if you like it and laugh at it at the same time."

These emotional and intellectual associations deepened Auden's dualism as well as his hopes of resolving it, and they inspired many of the themes of "The Sea and the Mirror," including its vision of the presexual innocence and unity of infancy and childhood, as well as its yearning for the sacramental union of the flesh and spirit in marriage, themes that recur in many of his other poems in the early 1940s. At the same time, though Auden yearned to transcend dualism—he said that "All the striving of life is a striving to transcend duality"—he remained acutely conscious of its contrapuntal manifestations in human existence. He said that in this world "all experience is dualistic," and insisted that "Man is neither pure spirit nor pure nature—if he were purely either he would have no history—but exists in and as a tension between their two opposing polarities." He thus praised what he called "binocular vision," and said that the "one infallible symptom of greatness is the capacity for double focus."

Counterpoint and double focus are apparent throughout "The Sea and the Mirror," including the Preface, a lyric that Auden wrote while he was composing "For the Time Being." The Preface presents a pervasive opposition between art and religious truth, between "the world of fact we love" and the reality of death, the "silence / On the other side of the wall." The Stage Manager contrasts the circus audience "wet with sympathy now" for the spectacle they see and the scriptural peril of "the lion's mouth whose hunger / No metaphors can fill"; and he suggests, as Shakespeare's Prospero does in his "Our revels now are ended" speech (4.1.148–58) and in his Epilogue, that the illusions of art are like the illusions of human life it imitates. Neither can reveal the process of moral choice "Between Shall-I and I-Will," and neither can quote the ultimate "smiling / Secret."

In Chapter I of the poem, in Prospero's speech to Ariel, which Auden described to Isherwood as "The Artist to his genius," Prospero presents a similarly divided view of art in a fallen world. He associates the childhood experience of "The gross insult of being a mere one among many" with the development of his magical power, "the power to enchant / That comes from disillusion," and he says that as we look into Ariel's "calm eyes, / With their lucid proof of apprehension and disorder, / All we are not stares back at what we are." Auden sees Prospero's character as itself paradoxical. In his 1954 essay on *The Tempest*, Auden deprecated Shakespeare's Prospero. He questioned his treatment of others, especially Caliban, and concluded, "He has the coldness of someone who has come to the conclusion that human nature is not worth much, that human relations are, at their best, pretty sorry affairs. . . . One might excuse him if he included himself in his critical skepticism but he never does; it never occurs to him that he, too, might have erred and be in need of pardon." In a list at the very beginning of his draft of "The Sea and the Mirror," Auden grouped the characters of *The Tempest*, as well as of his poem, with other characters in Shakespeare's plays they reminded him of—a critical practice he also recommended to students. In this list, he associated Prospero with Hamlet, a character whom he found unsympathetic, and whose self-absorption he criticized in his lectures. In the poem, Auden portrays Prospero as similarly self-absorbed; he also diminishes him by making the natural Caliban rather than the spiritual Ariel the spokesman for art and gracing Caliban with the sophisticated prose style of the later works of Henry James.

At the same time, Auden unquestionably identified profoundly with Prospero as an artist. In his 1947 lecture on *The Tempest*, which is more sympathetic to Shakespeare's Prospero and in this respect closer in spirit to "The Sea and the Mirror" than his later essays on the play, Auden emphasizes that art

> can give people an experience, but it cannot dictate the use they make of that experience. Alonso is reminded of his crime against Prospero, but he repents by himself. Ferdinand and Miranda are tested, but the quality of their love is their own. The bad are exposed and shown that crime doesn't pay, but they can't be made to give up their ambition. That art cannot thus transform men grieves Prospero greatly. His anger at Caliban stems from his consciousness of this failure. . . . You can hold the mirror up to a person, but you may make him worse.

The same consciousness of failure, the pained recognition, as he wrote in 1939 in his elegy to Yeats, that "poetry makes nothing happen," underlies Auden's depiction of Prospero in "The Sea and the Mirror." His Prospero also alludes to passages in Augustine and Kierkegaard that Auden particularly valued; his songs, the first especially, directly reflect Auden's searing experience with Chester Kallman; and the whole of his speech, in its poignancy and wit, suggests Auden's own voice. In his draft of "The Sea and the Mirror," as well as in a letter to Isherwood, Auden drew a diagram, derived from his Swarthmore chart and Alonso's speech, placing Prospero (Ego) in the world of Existence between the worlds of Actuality (or Immediacy) and of Possibility, the former represented by the Sea (Nature) and Caliban (Life), the latter by the Mirror (Art) and Ariel (Spirit). Prospero embodies all of these oppositions, and they are reflected in the way in which he talks, in the texture of his speech and songs—"resigning thoughts" and "revelling wishes"; "heavy books" and "words" that "carry no weight"; "A punctual plump judge, a fly-weight hermit"; "*witty angels who / Come only to the beasts*"; "Cold walls, hot spaces, wild mouths, defeated backs"; "moonshine and daylight"; "*this rough world*" and "*a smoother song.*"

Comparable oppositions animate the rest of "The Sea and the Mirror" as well. In Chapter II, the members of the supporting cast reveal themselves, on the deck of the ship taking them back to Naples, in a pyrotechnic variety of verse forms. The combination of Auden's own varied descriptions of these characters in the draft; Prospero's, Antonio's, and Caliban's comments on them; and their own speeches suggests that Auden conceived of them from multiple complementary and conflicting perspectives. Antonio, the first speaker, is represented as the intractable opponent of Prospero and his project of reconciliation and renewal. Like Iago, with whom Auden associated him and on whom he is in many respects modeled, he is a representation of the unregenerate will, a demonic outsider. Antonio is similarly significant in *The Tempest*, haunting the play and not speaking a word when Prospero grudgingly forgives him, but Auden's profound interest in the figure of the outsider gives his Antonio an imaginative consciousness that Shakespeare's Antonio does not have. He opens the chapter and punctuates it with responses to the speeches of each of the other characters, and he provides an insistent counterpoint to Prospero. He asserts

his own refractory existence as the necessary precondition of
Prospero's art:

> as long as I choose
>
> To wear my fashion, whatever you wear
> Is a magic robe; while I stand outside
> Your circle, the will to charm is still there.

He poses an antithesis between adulthood and the paradisal possi-
bilities of childhood from which Prospero is excluded:

> As I exist so you shall be denied,
> Forced to remain our melancholy mentor,
> The grown-up man, the adult in his pride,
>
> Never have time to curl up at the centre
> Time turns on when completely reconciled,
> Never become and therefore never enter
> The green occluded pasture as a child.

His speech concludes:

> *Your all is partial, Prospero;*
>   *My will is all my own:*
> *Your need to love shall never know*
> *Me: I am I, Antonio,*
>   *By choice myself alone.*

Antonio speaks a different variation on this final stanza as a coda to
the speeches of each of the other characters.

Ferdinand's lyrical sonnet to Miranda, which Auden described in
his draft as "mutuality of love begets love," expresses a serious mysti-
cal quest for "another tenderness," at the same time, Auden told
Isherwood, that it "describes fucking in completely abstract words,"
as later Caliban, the id, speaks abstractly, in a highly mannered
Jamesian style, about art. In both his draft and his letter to Isher-

wood, Auden compared Ferdinand and Miranda, probably with some amusement, to Milton's Adam and Eve: "Ferdinand: Masculine (He for God only)" and "Miranda: Feminine (She for God in him)"; and he grouped Ferdinand with Henry V and Mr. W. H., the presumed young man in the *Sonnets,* both of whom he deplored in his lectures on Shakespeare. Auden also has Caliban remarking, in an early version of his speech, that "Miranda and Ferdinand have spoken themselves to giants / Swooning in Egypt," an ironic allusion to Shakespeare's Antony and Cleopatra, lovers whose poetry Auden admired but whose romantic love he regarded as worldly pretension.

Auden associated Stephano with Falstaff and the "flight from anxiety into unconsciousness." Auden regarded anxiety as the condition of existence, and in his Swarthmore chart he placed it midway between the hell of sensuality on one hand and the hell of pride on the other. In his ballade, Stephano declares to his drinker's belly, which he variously addresses as "a bride," "Dear Daughter," "nanny," "Child," and "Mother," that "Where mind meets matter, both should woo." He hides behind its "skirts . . . / When disappointments bark and boo," and is comforted by it, as by a "Wise nanny" with her "vulgar pooh." But his retreat to drink and childhood reveals the adult division rather than the childhood unity of mind and body:

> Though in the long run satisfied,
> The will of one by being two
> At every moment is denied;
> Exhausted glasses wonder who
> Is self and sovereign, I or You?
> We cannot both be what we claim,
> The real Stephano—Which is true?
> A lost thing looks for a lost name.

The portrait of Gonzalo is explicitly paradoxical. Auden thought of him as akin to Polonius and as a "man who makes goodness easy by blinding himself to evil." Shakespeare depicts Gonzalo as a

slightly foolish but essentially "good old Lord" (5.1.15), an inno-
cent, the aged counterpart of Miranda. Auden's Gonzalo is a man
who "By his self-reflection made / Consolation an offence," who
"by speculation froze / Vision into an idea" and eventually "stood
convicted of / Doubt and insufficient love." His speech nonetheless
ends with another kind of paradox, as he draws upon the memory
of the imaginative consolations of his boyhood to redeem his old
age. Immediately following is the paradox of Adrian and Francisco's
camp lament: "Good little sunbeams must learn to fly" while "the
goldfish die."

Alonso's speech is composed entirely of antitheses. He is the most
penitent character in *The Tempest* and the one to whom Auden seems
to have been most profoundly drawn. Auden grouped him in his
draft with Henry IV, a similarly guilt-ridden and grief-stricken father
to whom Auden also responded with sympathy. Extending the Stage
Manager's image in the Preface of a couple walking a "tightrope,"
Alonso tells Ferdinand that "The Way of Justice is a tightrope /
Where no prince is safe for one instant." On one side of the tight-
rope is the sea of sensuality and lust, and on the other is the desert
of intellect and pride, an antinomy Auden elaborated in the con-
temporaneous Swarthmore chart as well as in *The Enchafèd Flood* in
1950. Alonso describes the opposing perils of the sea and the desert
at length and tells Ferdinand that he must find his way as a ruler
"Between the watery vagueness and / The triviality of the sand":

> But should you fail to keep your kingdom
> And, like your father before you, come
> Where thought accuses and feeling mocks,
> Believe your pain: praise the scorching rocks
> For their desiccation of your lust,
> Thank the bitter treatment of the tide
> For its dissolution of your pride,
> That the whirlwind may arrange your will

> And the deluge release it to find
> The spring in the desert, the fruitful
> Island in the sea, where flesh and mind
> Are delivered from mistrust.

The nostalgic song of the Master and Boatswain presents the irresolvable oppositions of a world where "The homeless played at keeping house," where grown men try to recover maternal love with "nightingales" (the same slang term for prostitutes used by T. S. Eliot in "Sweeney Among the Nightingales"):

> The nightingales are sobbing in
>   The orchards of our mothers,
> And hearts that we broke long ago
>   Have long been breaking others;
> Tears are round, the sea is deep:
> Roll them overboard and sleep.

The speech of Sebastian, whom Auden in a notebook entry initially associated with the character of Roderigo in *Othello*, also embodies an antithesis, though less obviously than Alonso's, the antithesis of adult and child. In adult consciousness, thought and act are separated in time and by their respective natures. Freud argued that in the animistic, magical thinking of infancy, however, there is no gap between the present intention and the future act, and the thought is equivalent to the deed. Freud considered this state at once an Eden that adults wish to recover and the source of their Oedipal guilt, since residues of infantile belief that the thought and the deed are one, that the wish to murder and the act of murder are the same, persist in adult life. In the speech of Sebastian Auden anatomizes such pre-Oedipal thinking:

> What sadness signalled to our children's day
> Where each believed all wishes wear a crown
> And anything pretended is alive,

> That one by one we plunged into that dream
> Of solitude and silence where no sword
> Will ever play once it is called a proof?

Sebastian had intended Alonso's death—"To think his death I thought myself alive"—but as Auden wrote in his draft as well as in a letter to Isherwood, he is "redeemed by failure," by the adult consciousness of the difference between thinking and acting. Part of the power of his sestina nonetheless rests in its depiction of a child's mind.

Trinculo's speech too, and more explicitly, depends upon the opposition of child and adult. Trinculo presents himself as "the cold clown / Whose head is in the clouds. . . . The north wind steals my hat," but he says that

> On clear days I can see
> Green acres far below,
> And the red roof where I
> Was Little Trinculo.

In the draft, Trinculo's speech focuses entirely on memories of childhood, and Auden grouped him with Shallow, the character in *Henry IV, Part Two* who is wholly defined by memories of his youth, as well as with Jaques's melancholy and the "flight from anxiety into wit."

Auden's interest in what Caliban calls "the green kingdom" of childhood had a religious foundation. Auden related the verse "Suffer little children, and forbid them not, to come unto me: for of such is the kingdom of heaven" (Matt. 19.14) to the most central tenets of his faith. He considered the verse an answer to "those who think of the good life as something contrary to our animal nature, that the flesh is not divine," as well as a statement of the human need, not only the injunction, to "love thy neighbour as thyself," since children, who "do love and trust their neighbour naturally unless their trust is betrayed," show that such love is part of our "biological nature." But Auden's attraction to childhood was also temperamental. Toward the end of his life he wrote in his commonplace book *A Certain World*, "I was both the youngest child and the youngest grandchild in my family. Being a fairly bright boy, I was generally the youngest in my school class. The result of this was that, until quite recently, I have always assumed that, in any gathering, I was the youngest person present."

Miranda's luminous villanelle, which Auden labeled "integrated love" in his draft, presents the joining of the mirror of art and the nature it reflects, the fundamental aesthetic duality of "The Sea and the Mirror," in a childlike apprehension of love and matrimony. Both Shakespeare's Prospero and Auden's are skeptical of the romantic hyperboles of Miranda and Ferdinand. Prospero says dryly to Miranda in *The Tempest* that Ferdinand's world seems "brave" to her only because of its novelty (5.1.183–84). Auden's Prospero asks, more pointedly,

> Will a Miranda who is
> No longer a silly lovesick little goose,
> When Ferdinand and his brave world are her profession,
> Go into raptures over existing at all?

In his lecture on *The Tempest*, Auden said that both Miranda and Ferdinand "are good but untempted and inexperienced—they think that love can produce Gonzalo's Utopia here and now." Miranda's verse nonetheless clearly celebrates the spiritual innocence of her fairy-tale feelings. She revisits Antonio's reference to the Eden of childhood, but with the "green pasture" no longer "occluded," and in the final stanza she speaks of the "changing garden," in which she and Ferdinand "Are linked as children in a circle dancing." Auden returned to the idea of children dancing in a ring of agape in a lecture at the New School in which he quoted a passage from Lewis Carroll's *Through the Looking Glass* that suggests an association of the image with the music of the spheres. The passage describes Alice dancing with Tweedledum and Tweedledee:

> . . . she took hold of both hands at once: the next moment they were dancing round in a ring. This seemed quite natural (she remembered afterwards), and she was not even surprised to hear music playing: it seemed to come from the tree under which they were dancing, and it was done (as well as she could make it out) by the branches rubbing one across the other, like fiddles and fiddlesticks. . . . "I don't know when I began it, but somehow I felt as if I had been singing it a long long time!"

Auden's conception of Caliban as well as of Ariel in Chapter III is the most radical expression of dualism in "The Sea and the Mirror." Speaking first on behalf of the audience, Caliban asks Shakespeare whether his definition of art as " 'a mirror held up to nature' " does not indicate the "mutual reversal of value" between the real and the imagined, since on "the far side of the mirror the general will to compose, to form at all costs a felicitous pattern becomes the *necessary cause* of any particular effort to live or act or love or triumph or vary, instead of being as, in so far as it emerges at all, it is on this side, their *accidental effect?*" Caliban asks Shakespeare how he could thus "be guilty of the incredible unpardonable treachery" of introducing him into his play, "the one creature" whom the Muse "will not under any circumstances stand," the child of "the unrectored chaos," "the represented principle of *not* sympathising, *not* associating, *not* amusing." He protests also, "Is it possible that, not content with inveigling Caliban into Ariel's kingdom, you have also let loose Ariel in Caliban's?" In the next section of the chapter, Caliban assumes his "officially natural role" to address those in the audience who wish to become writers. He describes how the writers in the audience finally master Ariel only to discover reflected in his eyes

"a gibbering fist-clenched creature with which you are all too un-
familiar . . . the only subject that you have, who is not a dream ame-
nable to magic but the all too solid flesh you must acknowledge as
your own; at last you have come face to face with me, and are ap-
palled to learn how far I am from being, in any sense, your dish."
In the final section of Chapter III, Caliban tells the audience that
he begins "to feel something of the serio-comic embarrassment of
the dedicated dramatist, who, in representing to you your condition
of estrangement from the truth, is doomed to fail the more he suc-
ceeds, for the more truthfully he paints the condition, the less
clearly can he indicate the truth from which it is estranged." Caliban
finally resolves this paradox by attempting to transcend it, by ac-
knowledging "that Wholly Other Life from which we are separated
by an essential emphatic gulf of which our contrived fissures of mir-
ror and proscenium arch—we understand them at last—are feebly
figurative signs."

The oppositions Caliban describes in his long prose speech are
also represented in his style, in the deliberately antithetical juxtapo-
sition of the flesh he embodies with the abstract language he uses.
Auden had played Caliban in a school play, he associated him with
Falstaff, the character in Shakespeare whom he most admired, and
he was particularly proud of the style of Caliban's speech in "The
Sea and the Mirror," a speech he considered his masterpiece. He
wrote to Spencer:

> Caliban does disturb me profoundly because he doesn't fit in;
> it is exactly as if one of the audience had walked onto the stage
> and insisted on taking part in the action. I've tried to work for
> this effect in a non-theatrical medium, by allowing the reader
> for the first two chapters not to think of the theatre (by inver-
> sion, therefore, to be witnessing a performance) and then sud-
> denly wake him up in one (again by inversion, introducing 'real
> life' into the imagined.)

This is putting one's head straight into the critics' mouths, for most of them will spot the James pastiche, say this is a piece of virtuosity, which it is, and unseemly levity or meaningless, which it isn't.

"Caliban is Ariel's Oracle," Auden continued, since Caliban, "as the personification of Nature, has the power of individuation, but no power of conception," whereas Ariel, "as the personification of Spirit, has the power of conception but not of individuation":

> What I was looking for was, therefore, (a) A freak 'original' style (Caliban's contribution), (b) a style as 'spiritual', as far removed from Nature, as possible (Ariel's contribution) and James seemed to fit the bill exactly, and not only for these reasons, but also because he is the great representative in English literature of what Shakespeare certainly was not, the 'dedicated artist' to whom art is religion. You cannot imagine him saying 'The best in this kind are but shadows' or of busting his old wand. In fact Ariel fooled him a little, hence a certain Calibanesque 'monstrosity' about his work.
>
> I have, as you say, a dangerous fondness for 'trucs' [ways around things, poetic tricks]; I've tried to turn this to advantage by selecting a subject where it is precisely the 'truc' that *is* the subject; the serious matter being the fundamental frivolity of art. I hope someone, besides yourself, will see this.

This conception of art is critical to all of Auden's later work, because it enabled him to distinguish and transform his taste for camp as well as "trucs." It helps account for his attraction to Kierkegaard's distinctions of the aesthetic, the ethical, and the religious, and it reflects his own deep religious commitment. In an address on Henry James to the Grolier Club in 1946, Auden remarked that "along with most human activities," art "is, in the profoundest sense, frivolous. For one thing, and one thing only, is serious: loving one's neighbor as one's self." In the letter to Spencer, Auden also wrote, "I'm extremely pleased and surprised to find that at least one reader feels that the section written in a pastiche of James is more me than the sections written in my own style, because it is the paradox I was trying for, and am afraid hardly anyone will get." In a review in 1944, Auden said that James "was not, like Mallarmé or Yeats, an esthete, but, like Pascal, one to whom, however infinitely various its circumstances, the interest itself of human life was always the single dreadful choice it offers, with no 'second chance,' of either salvation or damnation."

Shakespeare's representation of dualism in *The Tempest* is not governed by the Manichaeism Auden saw, though elements of it may be present, but by the tragicomic idea of *felix culpa*, the paradox of the fortunate fall, where good is consubstantial with evil, and can issue from it. At the outset of the action Prospero tells Miranda when she sees the shipwreck that there is "no harm done . . . No harm," and that he has "done nothing but in care of" her (1.2.14–16). His care culminates in her betrothal but evolves through her suffering as well as his own, and he associates that suffering with the blessing as well as pain of their exile from Milan. They were driven from the city, he tells her, "By foul play . . . / But blessedly holp hither" (1.2.62–64), sighing "To th' winds, whose pity, sighing back again, / Did us but loving wrong" (1.2.150–51). The same motif is expressed by Ferdinand as he submits to Prospero's rule and to the ritual ordeal that Prospero contrives to make him value the love of Miranda: "some kinds of baseness / Are nobly undergone, and most poor matters / Point to rich ends. . . . The mistress which I serve quickens what's dead / And makes my labours pleasures" (3.1.2–7). Gonzalo, summing up the whole action of the play, says that everyone has found himself "When no man was his own" (5.1.213).

Auden hints at a comparable kind of paradox, though more tenuously, in a number of the speeches of the supporting cast in Chapter

II of "The Sea and the Mirror," especially Sebastian's, as well as at
the end of Caliban's speech in Chapter III. The sense of resolved,
if not fortunate, suffering, however, is most fully developed in the
Postscript, where Ariel sings of his love for Caliban's mortality and
of its completion of his own spiritual being. Ariel speaks for the first
time in the poem, and is echoed by the Prompter, who suggests the
voice of Auden as well as that of Prospero:

> Weep no more but pity me,
> Fleet persistent shadow cast
> By your lameness, caught at last,
> Helplessly in love with you,
> Elegance, art, fascination,
>> Fascinated by
>> Drab mortality;
> Spare me a humiliation,
>> To your faults be true:
> I can sing as you reply
>>> . . . *I*

Ariel proposes a union of antitheses—"For my company be lonely /
For my health be ill: / I will sing if you will cry"—in which he and
Caliban will be joined not despite, but because of, the differences
between them.

Ariel's song ends with a reference to death, "One evaporating
sigh," a counterpart of Prospero's description in *The Tempest* of "our
little life . . . rounded with a sleep" (4.1.157–58) as well as of his
general preoccupation with last things. Shakespeare may have been
thinking of the liturgy of All Souls' Day when he wrote *The Tempest*,
and the play is in significant respects a meditation on death, which
may be one reason why many modern critics have found it essen-
tially different from Shakespeare's other last plays and more per-
turbing, and why Auden, writing in a time of war, with its "unmen-
tionable odour of death," should have found it so apposite. Alonso

and Gonzalo are old men; Prospero says starkly, "Every third thought shall be my grave" (5.1.311); and the contrast between youth and age is insistent in the play. Auden responds deeply to this undercurrent in *The Tempest,* and the representation in "The Sea and the Mirror" of old age and death against the perspective of childhood may be the dialectical opposition that moved him most. In the Preface, the Stage Manager begins by observing the aged catching their breath and children laughing, and ends by saying that "the Bard"

> Was sober when he wrote
> That this world of fact we love
> Is unsubstantial stuff:
> All the rest is silence
> On the other side of the wall;
> And the silence ripeness,
> And the ripeness all.

"The rest is silence" are Hamlet's last words (5.2.369); "Ripeness is all" are Edgar's words of benediction for his dying father Gloucester in *King Lear* (5.2.11); and "unsubstantial stuff" refers to Prospero's famous speech to Ferdinand describing the ending of the revels of life as well as of the masque in *The Tempest:*

> You do look, my son, in a mov'd sort,
> As if you were dismay'd. Be cheerful, sir.
> Our revels now are ended. These our actors,
> As I foretold you, were all spirits and
> Are melted into air, into thin air;
> And, like the baseless fabric of this vision,
> The cloud capp'd towers, the gorgeous palaces,
> The solemn temples, the great globe itself,
> Yea, all which it inherit, shall dissolve,
> And, like this insubstantial pageant faded,

Leave not a rack behind. We are such stuff
As dreams are made on, and our little life
Is rounded with a sleep.

(4.1.146–58)

In Chapter I of "The Sea and the Mirror," Prospero's whole speech is that of a man preparing himself for "the time death pounces / His stumping question." After freeing his Muse Ariel, "So at last I can really believe I shall die," he looks back on his childhood, youth, and life as an artist. He talks of the journey he must now take "inch by inch, / Alone and on foot," and dwells on the picture of himself as "an old man / Just like other old men, with eyes that water / Easily in the wind, and a head that nods in the sunshine." He refers to the Kierkegaardian spiritual voyage over "seventy thousand fathoms" and in his last lyric asks Ariel to sing "*Of separation, / Of bodies and death,*" as "*Trembling he takes / The silent passage / Into discomfort.*"

In Chapter II, Antonio invokes the green pasture of childhood and in his final lines describes

> *The figure that Antonio,*
> *The Only One, Creation's O*
> *Dances for Death alone.*

The subject of Sebastian's infantile thinking is death, his own as well as his brother Alonso's, and Trinculo's insistent memories of his childhood end with the wish for death:

> Wild images, come down
> Out of your freezing sky,
> That I, like shorter men,
> May get my joke and die.

The Master and Boatswain oppose the nostalgic memory of their mothers to the oblivion of the sea. In a different key, Gonzalo, also looking back to childhood, remembers "boyhoods growing and afraid" comforted by "Some ruined tower by the sea" (and by "the improbable stare / Of rocking horse and teddy bear" in the draft) and then turns to the solace of his "rusting flesh":

> A simple locus now, a bell
> The Already There can lay
> Hands on if at any time
> It should feel inclined to say
> To the lonely—"Here I am",
> To the anxious—"All is well".

Alonso, absorbed in the future life of his young son, says he is "now ready to welcome / Death, but rejoicing in a new love, / A new peace."

The resonance of such a love Auden would also have found in *The Tempest*. At the close of the play, in the Epilogue, Prospero pleads for the audience's charity as they themselves must pray for God's charity, and in the body of the play, in a climactic and well-known speech just before he renounces his art, he resolves to forgive his enemies. When Ariel tells him that his "affections" would "become tender" if he beheld the sufferings of the court party, Prospero answers:

> And mine shall.
> Hast thou, which art but air, a touch, a feeling
> Of their afflictions, and shall not myself,
> One of their kind, that relish all as sharply
> Passion as they, be kindlier moved than thou art?
> Though with their high wrongs I am struck to th' quick,
> Yet with my nobler reason 'gainst my fury
> Do I take part. The rarer action is
> In virtue than in vengeance.

(5.1.18–28)

This speech may not be one to which Auden especially attended in "The Sea and the Mirror," and he is likely to have found its elevation of reason to be symptomatic of the Manichaeism in *The Tempest* to which he objected, but the impulse to forgive is one that he deeply shared and that was always latent in his dualistic thinking. In his Swarthmore chart, it is the immediate prelude to Paradise. The idea of forgiveness is absent in the Preface by the Stage Manager but is present in muted form in Prospero's speech in Chapter I. Prospero, in Auden's presentation, speaks only briefly of forgiveness, and where Shakespeare's Prospero seems mistaken only about Caliban, not others, and is, arguably, finally charitable even toward Caliban—he "acknowledges" him as a part of himself (5.1.275–76), and Caliban for his part vows to be "wise hereafter, / And seek for grace" (5.1.294–95)—Auden's Prospero can seem ungenerous in his response to other characters as well. On the other hand, his irony does not exclude sympathy, and his judgments frequently echo Auden's own astringent labels for those characters in his draft and letters as well as comparable attitudes expressed elsewhere in his writing. Prospero's speech in "The Sea and the Mirror" depicts the disengagement of a man who is leaving life behind him, not altogether unlike Troilus's lines (which Auden admired) at the end of Chaucer's *Troilus and Criseyde*. His speech, also, is specifically an address to his Muse, and in the draft even the hostile Antonio recognizes, if sarcastically, that the purpose of Prospero's "conjuring" is gracious: "it's wonderful / Really, how much you have managed to do. . . . So they / Did want to better themselves after all / All over the ship I hear them pray / As loyal subjects, to be grateful enough, / Trying so hard to believe what you say / About life as a dream in search of grace / And to understand what you mean by the real." Prospero himself in the final text affirms rightly if dispassionately:

The extravagant children, who lately swaggered
Out of the sea like gods, have, I think, been soundly hunted
    By their own devils into their human selves:
To all, then, but me, their pardons.

Prospero may wonder how long Ferdinand and Miranda will remain
enraptured, but he says in addition that "Their eyes are big and blue
with love; its lighting / Makes even us look new," and adds, "Proba-
bly I over-estimate their difficulties." In the draft, he says more re-
vealingly, in a line in which Auden is perhaps glancing at his own
sexual nature, "I probably over-estimate these difficulties / For na-
tures less indirect than mine." In the published text, Prospero also
says, with the cadence of Auden's characteristic humor,

Just the same, I am very glad I shall never
Be twenty and have to go through that business again,
    The hours of fuss and fury, the conceit, the expense.

If the theme of forgiveness is subdued in the depiction of Pros-
pero, however, it is manifest in the speeches of the supporting cast
in Chapter II. Stephano talks explicitly of the "need for pardon" in
his attempt to find union with his belly, to join mind and matter, and
Sebastian experiences a "proof / Of mercy" that rejuvenates him. In
his draft Auden indicated "forgiveness" as the subject of Sebastian's
sestina, and among the six words he initially considered to end the
lines in the sestina were "give" and "get," terms he used in a lecture
on *Timon of Athens* to discriminate agape and eros. Gonzalo, in the
last stanza of his speech, says, "There is nothing to forgive," and in
the draft Auden added, "There is everything to bless." In Chapter
III, Caliban speaks to the young artist in the audience of "that music
which explains and pardons all," and of the need, "if possible and as
soon as possible, to forgive and forget the past." He closes his speech
by saying that in "the Wholly Other Life ... all our meanings are
reversed and it is precisely in its negative image of Judgement that

we can positively envisage Mercy," a traditional Christian conception of Mercy as the fulfillment of the Law that parallels the idea of the fortunate fall that runs through *The Tempest*. In the Postscript, finally, with its overtones of Auden's relation with Kallman, the Prompter's "*I*" evokes not only Prospero the artist but also all the individual human beings whom Ariel and Caliban allegorically compose, and suggests a marriage of the flesh and spirit in this world, and of Auden himself with his vocation, that is animated by forgiveness and love.

Alonso, perhaps the most moving character in *The Tempest*, speaks in his final lines in "The Sea and the Mirror" not only of his being ready to welcome death but of

> having heard the solemn
> Music strike and seen the statue move
> To forgive our illusion.

The reference is to the coming to life of Hermione's statue in Shakespeare's *The Winter's Tale* (5.3), which Auden, in his lecture on the play at the New School, saw as the finest of Shakespeare's reconciliation scenes and a perfect celebration of forgiveness. Auden's late addition of the line "To forgive our illusion"—it is not in the draft—is the most expansive of the numerous Shakespearean allusions in "The Sea and the Mirror," comprehending the poem's deepest religious impulses as well as its deepest inspiration in Shakespeare, radiating both inward to the illusion it creates and outward to the illusion it imitates, a luminous counterpart of Shakespeare's grave and beautiful epilogue to *The Tempest*, a distillation of the reconciliation of charity and art that Auden sought in the poem and in his life.

THE TEXT

Auden wrote "The Sea and the Mirror" from October 1942 to February 1944, while he was teaching at Swarthmore College. He had written "For the Time Being, A Christmas Oratorio" in the previous year, and the two poems were published together in the volume *For the Time Being* (New York: Random House, 1944; London: Faber and Faber, 1945), Auden placing "The Sea and the Mirror" first in the volume, though it was written later, because he thought that the secular, if religiously informed, examination of art in the poem should be a prelude to the manifestly religious representation of the Incarnation in "For the Time Being."

Auden began thinking of "The Sea and the Mirror" in August 1942, when he wrote its Preface, in many respects the germ of the poem. He started writing "The Sea and the Mirror" in October and appears to have completed Chapter I, "Prospero to Ariel," in November. On 5 January 1943, he sent to Chester Kallman a copy of a greatly extended version of Adrian and Francisco's couplet, printed in the notes of this edition as well as in the posthumous collection *As I Walked Out One Evening.* On 9 January 1943 Auden wrote Elizabeth Mayer, "My stuff about the Tempest is going quite nicely so far," and he enclosed "one little bit" for her to read, a copy of "Ferdinand's Song." He had more difficulty writing Chapter III, "Caliban to the Audience." On 17 July 1943 he wrote Mayer, "I struck oil this week on the last part of the Tempest stuff after a fruitless prospecting of 3 months." A letter written later to Theodore Spencer, probably 24 March 1944, suggests that his statement to Mayer was premature. He told Spencer, "From May to Oct, I was completely stuck with Chap III." On 17 February 1944, he wrote Mayer, "Yesterday I finished the Tempest book which I want to show you."

Auden's drafts of "The Sea and the Mirror" exist in two handwritten manuscripts: one, almost entirely devoted to the poem, in the Poetry and Rare Books Collection of the Library of the State University of New York at Buffalo; the other, a draft of "For the Time Being" that contains material Auden transposed to "The Sea and the Mirror," in the Henry W. and Albert A. Berg Collection of the New York Public Library. The Buffalo MS, a lined folio accountant's ledger, contains drafts of Prospero's speech, the speeches of the Supporting

Cast, and many false starts of Caliban's speech. The Berg MS, also a folio ledger, contains drafts of the Preface and Postscript, and of significant sections of both Prospero's and Caliban's speeches, including Prospero's final song, "Sing, Ariel, sing." The Berg Collection also holds the Random House galleys of the final text of "The Sea and the Mirror," with Auden's handwritten revisions on the galleys. The notes to this edition quote significant portions of the MS drafts as well as of the textual changes on the galleys.

"The Sea and the Mirror" was reprinted in *The Collected Poetry of W. H. Auden* (New York: Random House, 1945) and *Collected Longer Poems* (London: Faber and Faber, 1968; New York: Random House, 1969). The Preface was printed in *Atlantic*, under that title, in August 1944; "Sing Ariel, sing" was reprinted in *W. H. Auden: A Selection by the Author* (Harmondsworth: Penguin, 1958) as "Invocation to Ariel," as well as in *Collected Shorter Poems, 1927–1957* (London: Faber, 1966; New York: Random House, 1967) and *Selected Poems* (London: Faber, 1968). Alonso's speech, "Alonso to Ferdinand," was first printed in *Partisan Review,* September–October 1943. "Stephano's Song," "Trinculo's Song," "Alonso to Ferdinand," "Song of the Master and the Boatswain," "Miranda's Song," and "Caliban to the Audience" were reprinted in *W. H. Auden: A Selection*; and all of Chapter II was reprinted in *Selected Poems*.

The text of this edition is based on the first edition in *For the Time Being* (1944). The variants in the subsequent printed editions are minor. The present edition alters the American spelling and punctuation of the 1944 text in order to follow the British practice Auden used in his manuscripts: e.g., "honour" and "realise" instead of "honor" and "realize," and punctuation outside of instead of inside quotation marks. In the 1944 edition, as well as in letters he wrote at the time, Auden headed Prospero's, the Supporting Cast's, and Caliban's speeches as, respectively, Chapter I, Chapter II, and Chapter III. Subsequent editions used the Roman numerals only, but Auden's clear intent was to present the sections as narrative "chapters," as they are printed in this edition. On the galleys, Auden added asterisks in the spaces between the different sections of Caliban's speech, capitalized all personal pronouns referring to him and to Ariel, and indicated that he wished to italicize the opening section of the speech (Caliban's address to Shakespeare on behalf of the audience), as it is for the first time in this edition. A number of the proofreaders' corrections on the galleys, which were incorporated in the first and subsequent editions, contradict Auden's sometimes eccentric habits of punctuation (he often omitted a comma between consecutive adjectives or adverbs, for example), and Auden's usage has been restored in the present edition.

Auden's editor at Random House, Bennett Cerf, advised against the italics for the opening section of Caliban's speech and prevailed, but Auden continued to protest about another issue, the typography of the chapter headings. He wrote to Cerf on 13 June 1944: "Maybe you are right about the italics, though I think it would be clearer with them. About the chapter headings, however, my opinion is unchanged. It isnt that I dont realise that, as such things go, the fount is well designed. It's a matter of principle. You would never think of using such a fount for, say, 'The Embryology of the Elasmobranch Liver', so why use it for poetry? I feel strongly that 'aesthetic' books should not be put in a special class."

THE SEA AND
THE MIRROR

A Commentary on
Shakespeare's
The Tempest

And am I wrong to worship where
Faith cannot doubt nor Hope despair
Since my own soul can grant my prayer?
Speak, God of Visions, plead for me
And tell why I have chosen thee.

EMILY BRONTË

PREFACE

(The Stage Manager to the Critics)

The aged catch their breath,
For the nonchalant couple go
Waltzing across the tightrope
As if there were no death
Or hope of falling down;
The wounded cry as the clown
Doubles his meaning, and O
How the dear little children laugh
When the drums roll and the lovely
Lady is sawn in half.

O what authority gives
Existence its surprise?
Science is happy to answer
That the ghosts who haunt our lives
Are handy with mirrors and wire,
That song and sugar and fire,
Courage and come-hither eyes
Have a genius for taking pains.
But how does one think up a habit?
Our wonder, our terror remains.

Art opens the fishiest eye
To the Flesh and the Devil who heat
The Chamber of Temptation
Where heroes roar and die.
We are wet with sympathy now;
Thanks for the evening; but how
Shall we satisfy when we meet,

Between Shall-I and I-Will,
The lion's mouth whose hunger
No metaphors can fill?

Well, who in his own back yard
Has not opened his heart to the smiling
Secret he cannot quote?
Which goes to show that the Bard
Was sober when he wrote
That this world of fact we love
Is unsubstantial stuff:
All the rest is silence
On the other side of the wall;
And the silence ripeness,
And the ripeness all.

CHAPTER I

Prospero to Ariel

Stay with me, Ariel, while I pack, and with your first free act
  Delight my leaving; share my resigning thoughts
As you have served my revelling wishes: then, brave spirit,
  Ages to you of song and daring, and to me
Briefly Milan, then earth. In all, things have turned out better
  Than I once expected or ever deserved;
I am glad that I did not recover my dukedom till
  I do not want it; I am glad that Miranda
No longer pays me any attention; I am glad I have freed you,
  So at last I can really believe I shall die.
For under your influence death is inconceivable:
  On walks through winter woods, a bird's dry carcase
Agitates the retina with novel images,
  A stranger's quiet collapse in a noisy street
Is the beginning of much lively speculation,
  And every time some dear flesh disappears
What is real is the arriving grief; thanks to your service,
  The lonely and unhappy are very much alive.

But now all these heavy books are no use to me any more, for
  Where I go, words carry no weight: it is best,
Then, I surrender their fascinating counsel
  To the silent dissolution of the sea
Which misuses nothing because it values nothing;
  Whereas man overvalues everything
Yet, when he learns the price is pegged to his valuation,
  Complains bitterly he is being ruined which, of course, he is.
So kings find it odd they should have a million subjects
  Yet share in the thoughts of none, and seducers

[handwritten annotation: library, knowledge, thought do not matter]

Are sincerely puzzled at being unable to love
   What they are able to possess; so, long ago,
In an open boat, I wept at giving a city,
   Common warmth and touching substance, for a gift
In dealing with shadows. If age, which is certainly
   Just as wicked as youth, look any wiser,
It is only that youth is still able to believe
   It will get away with anything, while age
Knows only too well that it has got away with nothing:
   The child runs out to play in the garden, convinced
That the furniture will go on with its thinking lesson,
   Who, fifty years later, if he plays at all,
Will first ask its kind permission to be excused.

   When I woke into my life, a sobbing dwarf
Whom giants served only as they pleased, I was not what I seemed;
   Beyond their busy backs I made a magic
To ride away from a father's imperfect justice,
   Take vengeance on the Romans for their grammar,
Usurp the popular earth and blot out for ever
   The gross insult of being a mere one among many:
Now, Ariel, I am that I am, your late and lonely master,
   Who knows now what magic is;—the power to enchant
That comes from disillusion. What the books can teach one
   Is that most desires end up in stinking ponds,
But we have only to learn to sit still and give no orders,
   To make you offer us your echo and your mirror;
We have only to believe you, then you dare not lie;
   To ask for nothing, and at once from your calm eyes,
With their lucid proof of apprehension and disorder,
   All we are not stares back at what we are. For all things
In your company, can be themselves: historic deeds
   Drop their hauteur and speak of shabby childhoods

When all they longed for was to join in the gang of doubts
  Who so tormented them; sullen diseases
Forget their dreadful appearance and make silly jokes;
  Thick-headed goodness for once is not a bore.
No one but you had sufficient audacity and eyesight
  To find those clearings where the shy humiliations
Gambol on sunny afternoons, the waterhole to which
  The scarred rogue sorrow comes quietly in the small hours:
And no one but you is reliably informative on hell;
  As you whistle and skip past, the poisonous
Resentments scuttle over your unrevolted feet,
  And even the uncontrollable vertigo,
Because it can scent no shame, is unobliged to strike.

> *Could he but once see Nature as*
>   *In truth she is for ever,*
> *What oncer would not fall in love?*
> *Hold up your mirror, boy, to do*
>   *Your vulgar friends this favour:*
> *One peep, though, will be quite enough;*
>   *To those who are not true,*
> *A statue with no figleaf has*
>   *A pornographic flavour.*

> *Inform my hot heart straight away*
>   *Its treasure loves another,*
> *But turn to neutral topics then,*
> *Such as the pictures in this room,*
>   *Religion or the Weather;*
> *Pure scholarship in Where and When,*
>   *How Often and With Whom,*
> *Is not for Passion that must play*
>   *The Jolly Elder Brother.*

Be frank about our heathen foe,
For Rome will be a goner
If you soft-pedal the loud beast;
Describe in plain four-letter words
This dragon that's upon her:
But should our beggars ask the cost,
Just whistle like the birds;
Dare even Pope or Caesar know
The price of faith and honour?

To-day I am free and no longer need your freedom:
You, I suppose, will be off now to look for likely victims;
    Crowds chasing ankles, lone men stalking glory,
Some feverish young rebel among amiable flowers
    In consultation with his handsome envy,
A punctual plump judge, a fly-weight hermit in a dream
    Of gardens that time is for ever outside—
To lead absurdly by their self-important noses.
    Are you malicious by nature? I don't know.
Perhaps only incapable of doing nothing or of
    Being by yourself, and, for all your wry faces,
May secretly be anxious and miserable without
    A master to need you for the work you need.
Are all your tricks a test? If so, I hope you find, next time,
    Someone in whom you cannot spot the weakness
Through which you will corrupt him with your charm. Mine you did
    And me you have: thanks to us both, I have broken
Both of the promises I made as an apprentice;—
    To hate nothing and to ask nothing for its love.
All by myself I tempted Antonio into treason;   *taking the*
    However that could be cleared up; both of us know   *blame*
That both were in the wrong, and neither need be sorry:
    But Caliban remains my impervious disgrace.

We did it, Ariel, between us; you found on me a wish
    For absolute devotion; result—his wreck
That sprawls in the weeds and will not be repaired:
    My dignity discouraged by a pupil's curse,
I shall go knowing and incompetent into my grave.

    The extravagant children, who lately swaggered
Out of the sea like gods, have, I think, been soundly hunted
    By their own devils into their human selves:
To all, then, but me, their pardons. Alonso's heaviness
    Is lost; and weak Sebastian will be patient
In future with his slothful conscience—after all, it pays;
    Stephano is contracted to his belly, a minor
But a prosperous kingdom; stale Trinculo receives,
    Gratis, a whole fresh repertoire of stories, and
Our younger generation its independent joy.
    Their eyes are big and blue with love; its lighting
Makes even us look new: yes, to-day it all looks so easy.
    Will Ferdinand be as fond of a Miranda
Familiar as a stocking? Will a Miranda who is
    No longer a silly lovesick little goose,
When Ferdinand and his brave world are her profession,
    Go into raptures over existing at all?
Probably I over-estimate their difficulties;
    Just the same, I am very glad I shall never
Be twenty and have to go through that business again,
    The hours of fuss and fury, the conceit, the expense.

> Sing first that green remote Cockaigne
>   Where whiskey-rivers run,
> And every gorgeous number may
>   Be laid by anyone;
> For medicine and rhetoric
>   Lie mouldering on shelves,

While sad young dogs and stomach-aches
  Love no one but themselves.

Tell then of witty angels who
  Come only to the beasts,
Of Heirs Apparent who prefer
  Low dives to formal feasts;
For shameless Insecurity
  Prays for a boot to lick,
And many a sore bottom finds
  A sorer one to kick.

Wind up, though, on a moral note;—
  That Glory will go bang,
Schoolchildren shall co-operate,
  And honest rogues must hang;
Because our sound committee man
  Has murder in his heart:
But should you catch a living eye,
  Just wink as you depart.

Now our partnership is dissolved, I feel so peculiar:
  As if I had been on a drunk since I was born
And suddenly now, and for the first time, am cold sober,
  With all my unanswered wishes and unwashed days
Stacked up all round my life; as if through the ages I had dreamed
  About some tremendous journey I was taking,
Sketching imaginary landscapes, chasms and cities,
  Cold walls, hot spaces, wild mouths, defeated backs,
Jotting down fictional notes on secrets overheard
  In theatres and privies, banks and mountain inns,
And now, in my old age, I wake, and this journey really exists,
  And I have actually to take it, inch by inch,
Alone and on foot, without a cent in my pocket,

Through a universe where time is not foreshortened,
No animals talk, and there is neither floating nor flying.

When I am safely home, oceans away in Milan, and
Realise once and for all I shall never see you again,
   Over there, maybe, it won't seem quite so dreadful
Not to be interesting any more, but an old man
   Just like other old men, with eyes that water
Easily in the wind, and a head that nods in the sunshine,
   Forgetful, maladroit, a little grubby,
And to like it. When the servants settle me into a chair
   In some well-sheltered corner of the garden,
And arrange my muffler and rugs, shall I ever be able
   To stop myself from telling them what I am doing,—
Sailing alone, out over seventy thousand fathoms—?
   Yet if I speak, I shall sink without a sound
Into unmeaning abysses. Can I learn to suffer
   Without saying something ironic or funny
On suffering? I never suspected the way of truth
   Was a way of silence where affectionate chat
Is but a robbers' ambush and even good music
   In shocking taste; and you, of course, never told me.
If I peg away at it honestly every moment,
   And have luck, perhaps by the time death pounces
His stumping question, I shall just be getting to know
   The difference between moonshine and daylight. . . .
I see you starting to fidget. I forgot. To you
   That doesn't matter. My dear, here comes Gonzalo
With a solemn face to fetch me. O Ariel, Ariel,
   How I shall miss you. Enjoy your element. Good-bye.

       Sing, Ariel, sing,
       Sweetly, dangerously
       Out of the sour

And shiftless water,
Lucidly out
Of the dozing tree,
Entrancing, rebuking
The raging heart
With a smoother song
Than this rough world,
Unfeeling god.

O brilliantly, lightly,
Of separation,
Of bodies and death,
Unanxious one, sing
To man, meaning me,
As now, meaning always,
In love or out,
Whatever that mean,
Trembling he takes
The silent passage
Into discomfort.

CHAPTER II

The Supporting Cast
(Sotto Voce)

ANTONIO

As all the pigs have turned back into men
And the sky is auspicious and the sea
Calm as a clock, we can all go home again.

Yes, it undoubtedly looks as if we
Could take life as easily now as tales
Write ever-after: not only are the

Two heads silhouetted against the sails
—And kissing of course—well-built, but the lean
Fool is quite a person, the fingernails

Of the dear old butler for once quite clean,
And the royal passengers quite as good
As rustics, perhaps better, for they mean

What they say, without, as a rustic would,
Casting reflections on the courtly crew.
Yes, Brother Prospero, your grouping could

Not be more effective: given a few
Incomplete objects and a nice warm day,
What a lot a little music can do.

Dotted about the deck they doze or play,
Your loyal subjects all, grateful enough
To know their place and believe what you say.

What lies
does he think
he's told?

Antonio, sweet brother, has to laugh.
How easy you have made it to refuse
Peace to your greatness! Break your wand in half,

The fragments will join; burn your books or lose
Them in the sea, they will soon reappear,
Not even damaged: as long as I choose

To wear my fashion, whatever you wear
Is a magic robe; while I stand outside
Your circle, the will to charm is still there.

As I exist so you shall be denied,
Forced to remain our melancholy mentor,
The grown-up man, the adult in his pride,

Never have time to curl up at the centre
Time turns on when completely reconciled,
Never become and therefore never enter
The green occluded pasture as a child.

Antonio craves his individuality

> *Your all is partial, Prospero;*
> *My will is all my own:*
> *Your need to love shall never know*
> *Me: I am I, Antonio,*
> *By choice myself alone.*

FERDINAND

Flesh, fair, unique, and you, warm secret that my kiss
Follows into meaning Miranda, solitude
Where my omissions are, still possible, still good,
Dear Other at all times, retained as I do this,

From moment to moment as you enrich them so
Inherit me, my cause, as I would cause you now

With mine your sudden joy, two wonders as one vow
Pre-empting all, here, there, for ever, long ago.

I would smile at no other promise than touch, taste, sight,
Were there not, my enough, my exaltation, to bless
As world is offered world, as I hear it to-night

Pleading with ours for us, another tenderness
That neither without either could or would possess,
The Right Required Time, The Real Right Place, O Light.

> *One bed is empty, Prospero,*
> *My person is my own;*
> *Hot Ferdinand will never know*
> *The flame with which Antonio*
> *Burns in the dark alone.*

STEPHANO

Embrace me, belly, like a bride;
Dear daughter, for the weight you drew
From humble pie and swallowed pride,
Believe the boast in which you grew:
Where mind meets matter, both should woo;
Together let us learn that game
The high play better than the blue:
A lost thing looks for a lost name.

Behind your skirts your son must hide
When disappointments bark and boo;
Brush my heroic ghosts aside,
Wise nanny, with a vulgar pooh:
Exchanging cravings we pursue
Alternately a single aim:
Between the bottle and the loo
A lost thing looks for a lost name.

Though in the long run satisfied,
The will of one by being two
At every moment is denied;
Exhausted glasses wonder who
Is self and sovereign, I or You?
We cannot both be what we claim,
The real Stephano—Which is true?
A lost thing looks for a lost name.

Child? Mother? Either grief will do;
The need for pardon is the same,
The contradiction is not new:
A lost thing looks for a lost name.

> *One glass is untouched, Prospero,*
>   *My nature is my own;*
> *Inert Stephano does not know*
> *The feast at which Antonio*
>   *Toasts One and One alone.*

GONZALO

Evening, grave, immense, and clear,
Overlook our ship whose wake
Lingers undistorted on
Sea and silence; I look back
For the last time as the sun
Sets behind that island where
All our loves were altered: yes,
My prediction came to pass,
Yet I am not justified,
And I weep but not with pride.
Not in me the credit for
Words I uttered long ago

Whose glad meaning I betrayed;
Truths to-day admitted, owe
Nothing to the councillor
In whose booming eloquence
Honesty became untrue.
Am I not Gonzalo who
By his self-reflection made
Consolation an offence?

There was nothing to explain:
Had I trusted the Absurd
And straightforward note by note
Sung exactly what I heard,
Such immediate delight
Would have taken there and then
Our common welkin by surprise,
All would have begun to dance
Jigs of self-deliverance.
It was I prevented this,
Jealous of my native ear,
Mine the art which made the song
Sound ridiculous and wrong,
I whose interference broke
The gallop into jog-trot prose
And by speculation froze
Vision into an idea,
Irony into a joke,
Till I stood convicted of
Doubt and insufficient love.

Farewell, dear island of our wreck:
All have been restored to health,
All have seen the Commonwealth,
There is nothing to forgive.

Since a storm's decision gave
His subjective passion back
To a meditative man,
Even reminiscence can
Comfort ambient troubles like
Some ruined tower by the sea
Whence boyhoods growing and afraid
Learn a formula they need
In solving their mortality,
Even rusting flesh can be
A simple locus now, a bell
The Already There can lay
Hands on if at any time
It should feel inclined to say
To the lonely—"Here I am",
To the anxious—"All is well".

One tongue is silent, Prospero,
My language is my own;
Decayed Gonzalo does not know
The shadow that Antonio
Talks to, at noon, alone.

ADRIAN *AND* FRANCISCO

Good little sunbeams must learn to fly,
But it's madly ungay when the goldfish die.

One act is censored, Prospero,
My audience is my own;
Nor Adrian nor Francisco know
The drama that Antonio
Plays in his head alone.

ALONSO

Dear Son, when the warm multitudes cry,
Ascend your throne majestically,
But keep in mind the waters where fish
See sceptres descending with no wish
To touch them; sit regal and erect,
But imagine the sands where a crown
Has the status of a broken-down
Sofa or mutilated statue:
Remember as bells and cannon boom
The cold deep that does not envy you,
The sunburnt superficial kingdom
Where a king is an object.

Expect no help from others, for who
Talk sense to princes or refer to
The scorpion in official speeches
As they unveil some granite Progress
Leading a child and holding a bunch
Of lilies? In their Royal Zoos the
Shark and the octopus are tactfully
Omitted; synchronised clocks march on
Within their powers: without, remain
The ocean flats where no subscription
Concerts are given, the desert plain
Where there is nothing for lunch.

Only your darkness can tell you what
A prince's ornate mirror dare not,
Which you should fear more—the sea in which
A tyrant sinks entangled in rich
Robes while a mistress turns a white back
Upon his splutter, or the desert

Where an emperor stands in his shirt
While his diary is read by sneering
Beggars, and far off he notices
A lean horror flapping and hopping
Toward him with inhuman swiftness:
Learn from your dreams what you lack,

For as your fears are, so must you hope.
The Way of Justice is a tightrope
Where no prince is safe for one instant
Unless he trust his embarrassment,
As in his left ear the siren sings
Meltingly of water and a night
Where all flesh had peace, and on his right
The efreet offers a brilliant void
Where his mind could be perfectly clear
And all his limitations destroyed:
Many young princes soon disappear
To join all the unjust kings.

So, if you prosper, suspect those bright
Mornings when you whistle with a light
Heart. You are loved; you have never seen
The harbour so still, the park so green,
So many well-fed pigeons upon
Cupolas and triumphal arches,
So many stags and slender ladies
Beside the canals. Remember when
Your climate seems a permanent home
For marvellous creatures and great men,
What griefs and convulsions startled Rome,
Ecbatana, Babylon.

How narrow the space, how slight the chance
For civil pattern and importance
Between the watery vagueness and
The triviality of the sand,
How soon the lively trip is over
From loose craving to sharp aversion,
Aimless jelly to paralysed bone:
At the end of each successful day
Remember that the fire and the ice
Are never more than one step away
From the temperate city; it is
But a moment to either.

But should you fail to keep your kingdom
And, like your father before you, come
Where thought accuses and feeling mocks,
Believe your pain: praise the scorching rocks
For their desiccation of your lust,
Thank the bitter treatment of the tide
For its dissolution of your pride,
That the whirlwind may arrange your will
And the deluge release it to find
The spring in the desert, the fruitful
Island in the sea, where flesh and mind
Are delivered from mistrust.

Blue the sky beyond her humming sail
As I sit to-day by our ship's rail
Watching exuberant porpoises
Escort us homeward and writing this
For you to open when I am gone:
Read it, Ferdinand, with the blessing
Of Alonso, your father, once King

Of Naples, now ready to welcome
Death, but rejoicing in a new love,
A new peace, having heard the solemn
Music strike and seen the statue move
To forgive our illusion.

> *One crown is lacking, Prospero,*
>   *My empire is my own;*
> *Dying Alonso does not know*
> *The diadem Antonio*
>   *Wears in his world alone.*

MASTER *AND* BOATSWAIN

At Dirty Dick's and Sloppy Joe's
  We drank our liquor straight,
Some went upstairs with Margery,
  And some, alas, with Kate;
And two by two like cat and mouse
The homeless played at keeping house.

There Wealthy Meg, the Sailor's Friend,
  And Marion, cow-eyed,
Opened their arms to me but I
  Refused to step inside;
I was not looking for a cage
In which to mope in my old age.

The nightingales are sobbing in
  The orchards of our mothers,
And hearts that we broke long ago
  Have long been breaking others;
Tears are round, the sea is deep:
Roll them overboard and sleep.

One gaze points elsewhere, Prospero,
My compass is my own;
Nostalgic sailors do not know
The waters where Antonio
Sails on and on alone.

SEBASTIAN

My rioters all disappear, my dream
Where Prudence flirted with a naked sword,
Securely vicious, crumbles; it is day;
Nothing has happened; we are all alive:
I am Sebastian, wicked still, my proof
Of mercy that I wake without a crown.

What sadness signalled to our children's day
Where each believed all wishes wear a crown
And anything pretended is alive,
That one by one we plunged into that dream
Of solitude and silence where no sword
Will ever play once it is called a proof?

The arrant jewel singing in his crown
Persuaded me my brother was a dream
I should not love because I had no proof,
Yet all my honesty assumed a sword;
To think his death I thought myself alive
And stalked infected through the blooming day.

The lie of Nothing is to promise proof
To any shadow that there is no day
Which cannot be extinguished with some sword,
To want and weakness that the ancient crown
Envies the childish head, murder a dream
Wrong only while its victim is alive.

O blessed be bleak Exposure on whose sword,
Caught unawares, we prick ourselves alive!
Shake Failure's bruising fist! Who else would crown
Abominable error with a proof?
I smile because I tremble, glad to-day
To be ashamed, not anxious, not a dream.

Children are playing, brothers are alive,
And not a heart or stomach asks for proof
That all this dearness is no lovers' dream;
Just Now is what it might be every day,
Right Here is absolute and needs no crown,
Ermine or trumpets, protocol or sword.

In dream all sins are easy, but by day
It is defeat gives proof we are alive;
The sword we suffer is the guarded crown.

> *One face cries nothing, Prospero,*
> *My conscience is my own;*
> *Pallid Sebastian does not know*
> *The dream in which Antonio*
> *Fights the white bull alone.*

TRINCULO

Mechanic, merchant, king,
Are warmed by the cold clown
Whose head is in the clouds
And never can get down.

Into a solitude
Undreamed of by their fat
Quick dreams have lifted me;
The north wind steals my hat.

On clear days I can see
Green acres far below,
And the red roof where I
Was Little Trinculo.

There lies that solid world
These hands can never reach;
My history, my love,
Is but a choice of speech.

A terror shakes my tree,
A flock of words fly out,
Whereat a laughter shakes
The busy and devout.

Wild images, come down
Out of your freezing sky,
That I, like shorter men,
May get my joke and die.

One note is jarring, Prospero,
  My humour is my own;
Tense Trinculo will never know
The paradox Antonio
  Laughs at, in woods, alone.

MIRANDA

My Dear One is mine as mirrors are lonely,
As the poor and sad are real to the good king,
And the high green hill sits always by the sea.

Up jumped the Black Man behind the elder tree,
Turned a somersault and ran away waving;
My Dear One is mine as mirrors are lonely.

The Witch gave a squawk; her venomous body
Melted into light as water leaves a spring,
And the high green hill sits always by the sea.

At his crossroads, too, the Ancient prayed for me;
Down his wasted cheeks tears of joy were running:
My Dear One is mine as mirrors are lonely.

He kissed me awake, and no one was sorry;
The sun shone on sails, eyes, pebbles, anything,
And the high green hill sits always by the sea.

So, to remember our changing garden, we
Are linked as children in a circle dancing:
My Dear One is mine as mirrors are lonely,
And the high green hill sits always by the sea.

> *One link is missing, Prospero,*
> *My magic is my own;*
> *Happy Miranda does not know*
> *The figure that Antonio,*
> *The Only One, Creation's O*
> *Dances for Death alone.*

CHAPTER III

Caliban to the Audience

If now, having dismissed your hired impersonators with verdicts ranging from the laudatory orchid to the disgusted and disgusting egg, you ask and, of course, notwithstanding the conscious fact of his irrevocable absence, you instinctively *do* ask for our so good, so great, so dead author to stand before the finally lowered curtain and take his shyly responsible bow for this, his latest, ripest production, it is I—my reluctance is, I can assure you, co-equal with your dismay— who will always loom thus wretchedly into your confused picture, for, in default of the all-wise, all-explaining master you would speak *to*, who else at least can, who else indeed must respond to your bewildered cry, but its very echo, the begged question you would speak to him *about*.

*   *   *

We must own [for the present I speak your echo] *to a nervous perplexity not unmixed, frankly, with downright resentment. How* can *we grant the indulgence for which in his epilogue your personified type of the creative so lamely, tamely pleaded? Imprisoned, by you, in the mood doubtful, loaded, by you, with distressing embarrassments, we are, we submit, in no position to set anyone free.*

Our native Muse, heaven knows and heaven be praised, is not exclusive. Whether out of the innocence of a childlike heart to whom all things are pure, or with the serenity of a status so majestic that the mere keeping up of tones and appearances, the suburban wonder as to what the strait-laced Unities might possibly think, or sad sour Probability possibly say, are questions for which she doesn't because she needn't, she hasn't in her lofty maturity any longer to care a rap, she invites, dear generous-hearted creature that she is, just tout le monde to drop in at any time so that her famous, memorable, sought-after evenings present to the speculative eye an ever-shining, never-tarnished proof of her amazing unheard-of power to combine and happily contrast, to make every shade of the social and moral palette contribute to the general richness, of the skill, unapproached and unattempted by Grecian aunt or Gallic sister, with which she can skate full tilt toward the forbidden incoherence and then, in the last split second, on the shuddering edge of the bohemian standardless abyss, effect her breathtaking triumphant turn.

No timid segregation by rank or taste for her, no prudent listing into those who will, who might, who certainly would not get on, no nicely graded scale of invitations to heroic formal Tuesdays, young comic Thursdays, al fresco farcical Saturdays. No, the real, the only, test of the theatrical as of the gastronomic, her practice confidently wagers, is the mixed perfected brew.

As he looks in on her, so marvellously at home with all her cosy swarm about her, what accents will not assault the new arrival's ear, the magnificent tropes of tragic defiance and despair, the repartee of the high humour, the pun of the very low, cultured drawl and manly illiterate bellow, yet all of them gratefully doing their huge or tiny best to make the party go?

And if, assured by her smiling wave that of course he may, he should presently set out to explore her vast and rambling mansion, to do honour to its dear odd geniuses of local convenience and proportion, its multiplied deities of mysterious stair and interesting alcove, not one of the laughing groups and engrossed warmed couples that he keeps "surprising"—the never-ending surprise for him is that he doesn't seem to—but affords some sharper instance of relations he would have been the last to guess at, choleric prince at his ease with lymphatic butler, moist hand-taking so to dry, youth getting on quite famously with stingy cold old age, some stranger vision of the large loud liberty violently rocking yet never, he is persuaded, finally upsetting the jolly crowded boat.

What, he may well ask, has the gracious goddess done to all these people that, at her most casual hint, they should so trustingly, so immediately take off those heavy habits one thinks of them as having for their health and happiness day and night to wear, without in this unfamiliar unbuttoned state—the notable absence of the slightest shiver or not-quite-inhibited sneeze is indication positive—for a second feeling the draught? Is there, could there be, any miraculous suspension of the wearily historic, the dingily geographic, the dully drearily sensible beyond her faith, her charm, her love, to command? Yes, there could be, yes, alas, indeed yes, O there is, right here, right now before us, the situation present.

How could you, you who are one of the oldest habitués at these delightful functions, one, possibly the closest, of her trusted inner circle, how could you be guilty of the incredible unpardonable treachery of bringing along the one creature, as you above all men must have known, whom she cannot and will not under any circumstances stand, the solitary exception she is not at any hour of the day or night at home to, the unique case that her attendant spirits have absolute instructions never, neither at the front door nor at the back, to admit?

At Him and at Him only does she draw the line, not because there are any limits to her sympathy but precisely because there are none. Just because of all she is and all she means to be, she cannot conceivably tolerate in her presence the represented principle of not sympathising, not associating, not amusing, the only child of her Awful Enemy, the rival whose real name she will never sully her lips with—"that envious witch" is sign sufficient—who does not rule but defiantly is the unrectored chaos.

All along and only too well she has known what would happen if, by any careless mischance—of conscious malice she never dreamed till now—He should ever manage to get in. She foresaw what He would do to the conversation, lying in wait for its vision of private love or public justice to warm to an Egyptian brilliance and then with some fishlike odour or bruit insolite snatching the visionaries back tongue-tied and blushing to the here and now; she foresaw what He would do to the arrangements, breaking, by a refusal to keep in step, the excellent order of the dancing ring, and ruining supper by knocking over the loaded appetising tray; worst of all, she foresaw, she dreaded, what He would end up by doing to her, that, not content with upsetting her guests, with spoiling their fun, His progress from outrage to outrage would not relent before the gross climax of His making, horror unspeakable, a pass at her virgin self.

Let us suppose, even, that in your eyes she is by no means as we have always fondly imagined, your dear friend, that what we have just witnessed was not what it seemed to us, the inexplicable betrayal of a life-long sacred loyalty, but your long-premeditated just revenge, the final evening up of some ancient never-forgotten score, then even so, why make us suffer who have never, in all conscience, done you harm? Surely the theatrical relation, no less than the marital, is governed by the sanely decent general law that, before visitors, in front of the children or the servants, there shall be no indiscreet revelation of animosity, no "scenes", that, no matter to what intolerable degrees of internal temperature and pressure restraint may raise both the injured and the guilty, nevertheless such restraint is applied to tones and topics, the exhibited picture must be still as always the calm and smiling one the most malicious observer can see nothing wrong with, and not until the last of those whom manifested anger or mistrust would embarrass or amuse or not be good for have gone away or out or up, is the voice raised, the table thumped, the suspicious letter snatched at or the outrageous bill furiously waved.

For we, after all—you cannot have forgotten this—are strangers to her. We have never claimed her acquaintance, knowing as well as she that we do not and never could belong on her side of the curtain. All we have ever asked for is that for a few hours the curtain should be left undrawn, so as to allow our humble ragged selves the privilege of craning and gaping at the splendid goings-on inside. We most emphatically do not ask that she should speak to us, or try to understand us; on the contrary our one desire has always been that she should preserve for ever her old high strangeness, for what delights us about her world is just that it neither is nor possibly could become one in which we could breathe or behave, that in her house the right of innocent passage should remain so universal that the same neutral space accommodates the conspirator and his victim, the generals of both armies, the chorus of patriots and the choir of nuns, palace and farmyard, cathedral and smugglers' cave, that time should never revert to that intransigent element we are so ineluctably and only too familiarly in, but remain the passive good-

natured creature she and her friends can by common consent do anything they like with—(it is not surprising that they should take advantage of their strange power and so frequently skip hours and days and even years: the dramatic mystery is that they should always so unanimously agree upon exactly how many hours and days and years to skip)—that upon their special constitutions the moral law should continue to operate so exactly that the timid not only deserve but actually win the fair, and it is the socially and physically unemphatic David who lays low the gorilla-chested Goliath with one well-aimed custard pie, that in their blessed climate, the manifestation of the inner life should always remain so easy and habitual that a sudden eruption of musical and metaphorical power is instantly recognized as standing for grief and disgust, an elegant contrapposto for violent death, and that consequently the picture which they in there present to us out here is always that of the perfectly tidiable case of disorder, the beautiful and serious problem exquisitely set without a single superfluous datum and insoluble with less, the expert landing of all the passengers with all their luggage safe and sound in the best of health and spirits and without so much as a scratch or a bruise.

Into that world of freedom without anxiety, sincerity without loss of vigour, feeling that loosens rather than ties the tongue, we are not, we re-iterate, so blinded by presumption to our proper status and interest as to expect or even wish at any time to enter, far less to dwell there.

Must we—it seems oddly that we must—remind you that our existence does not, like hers, enjoy an infinitely indicative mood, an eternally present tense, a limitlessly active voice, for in our shambling, slovenly makeshift world any two persons, whether domestic first or neighbourly second, require and necessarily presuppose in both their numbers and in all their cases, the whole inflected gamut of an alien third, since, without a despised or dreaded Them to turn the back on, there could be no intimate or affectionate Us to turn the eye to; that, chez nous, *Space is never the whole uninhibited circle but always some segment, its eminent domain upheld by two co-ordinates. There always has been and always will be not only the vertical boundary, the river on this side of which initiative and honesty stroll arm in arm wear-*

*ing sensible clothes, and beyond which is a savage elsewhere swarming with
contagious diseases, but also its horizontal counterpart, the railroad above
which houses stand in their own grounds, each equipped with a garage and
a beautiful woman, sometimes with several, and below which huddled shacks
provide a squeezing shelter to collarless herds who eat blancmange and have
never said anything witty. Make the case as special as you please; take the
tamest congregation or the wildest faction; take, say, a college. What river
and railroad did for the grosser instance, lawn and corridor do for the more
refined, dividing the tender who value from the tough who measure, the su-
perstitious who still sacrifice to causation from the heretics who have already
reduced the worship of truth to bare description, and so creating the academic
fields to be guarded with umbrella and learned periodical against the trespass
of any unqualified stranger, not a whit less jealously than the game-preserve
is protected from the poacher by the unamiable shot-gun. For without these
prohibitive frontiers we should never know who we were or what we wanted.
It is they who donate to neighbourhood all its accuracy and vehemence. It is
thanks to them that we do know with whom to associate, make love, exchange
recipes and jokes, go mountain climbing or sit side by side fishing from piers.
It is thanks to them, too, that we know against whom to rebel. We can shock
our parents by visiting the dives below the railroad tracks, we can amuse
ourselves on what would otherwise have been a very dull evening indeed, in
plotting to seize the post-office across the river.*

*Of course these several private regions must together comprise one public
whole—we would never deny that logic and instinct require that. Of course,
We and They are united in the candid glare of the same commercial hope by
day, and the soft refulgence of the same erotic nostalgia by night but—and
this is our point—without our privacies of situation, our local idioms of
triumph and mishap, our different doctrines concerning the transubstantia-
tion of the larger pinker bun on the terrestrial dish for which the mature sense
may reasonably water and the adult fingers furtively or unabashedly go for,
our specific choices of which hill it would be romantic to fly away over or
what sea it would be exciting to run away to, our peculiar visions of the
absolute stranger with a spontaneous longing for the lost who will adopt our*

misery not out of desire but pure compassion, without, in short, our devoted pungent expression of the partial and contrasted, the Whole would have no importance and its Day and Night no interest.

So, too, with Time who, in our auditorium, is not her dear old buffer so anxious to please everybody, but a prim magistrate whose court never adjourns, and from whose decisions, as he laconically sentences one to loss of hair and talent, another to seven days' chastity, and a third to boredom for life, there is no appeal. We should not be sitting here now, washed, warm, well-fed, in seats we have paid for, unless there were others who are not here; our liveliness and good-humour, such as they are, are those of survivors, conscious that there are others who have not been so fortunate, others who did not succeed in navigating the narrow passage or to whom the natives were not friendly, others whose streets were chosen by the explosion or through whose country the famine turned aside from ours to go, others who failed to repel the invasion of bacteria or to crush the insurrection of their bowels, others who lost their suit against their parents or were ruined by wishes they could not adjust or murdered by resentments they could not control; aware of some who were better and bigger but from whom, only the other day, Fortune withdrew her hand in sudden disgust, now nervously playing chess with drunken sea-captains in sordid cafés on the equator or the Arctic Circle, or lying, only a few blocks away, strapped and screaming on iron beds or dropping to naked pieces in damp graves. And shouldn't you too, dear master, reflect—forgive us for mentioning it—that we might very well not have been attending a production of yours this evening, had not some other and maybe—who can tell?—brighter talent married a barmaid or turned religious and shy or gone down in a liner with all his manuscripts, the loss recorded only in the corner of some country newspaper below A Poultry Lover's Jottings?

You yourself, we seem to remember, have spoken of the conjured spectacle as "a mirror held up to nature", a phrase misleading in its aphoristic sweep but indicative at least of one aspect of the relation between the real and the imagined, their mutual reversal of value, for isn't the essential artistic strangeness to which your citation of the sinisterly biassed image would point just this: that on the far side of the mirror the general will to compose, to form at all costs a felicitous pattern becomes the necessary cause *of any particular effort to live or act or love or triumph or vary, instead of being as, in so far as it emerges at all, it is on this side, their* accidental effect?

Does Ariel—to nominate the spirit of reflection in your terms—call for manifestation? Then neither modesty nor fear of reprisals excuses the one so called on from publicly confessing that she cheated at croquet or that he committed incest in a dream. Does He demand concealment? Then their nearest and dearest must be deceived by disguises of sex and age which anywhere else would at once attract the attentions of the police or the derisive whistle of the awful schoolboy. That is the price asked, and how promptly and gladly paid, for universal reconciliation and peace, for the privilege of all galloping together past the finishing post neck and neck.

How then, we continue to wonder, knowing all this, could you act as if you did not, as if you did not realise that the embarrassing compresence of the absolutely natural, incorrigibly right-handed, and, to any request for cooperation, utterly negative, with the enthusiastically self-effacing would be a simultaneous violation of both worlds, as if you were not perfectly well aware that the magical musical condition, the orphic spell that turns the fierce dumb greedy beasts into grateful guides and oracles who will gladly take one anywhere and tell one everything free of charge, is precisely and simply that of his finite immediate note not, *under any circumstances, being struck, of its not being tentatively whispered, far less positively banged.*

Are we not bound to conclude, then, that, whatever snub to the poetic you may have intended incidentally to administer, your profounder motive in so introducing Him to them among whom, because He doesn't belong, He couldn't appear as anything but His distorted parody, a deformed and savage slave, was to deal a mortal face-slapping insult to us among whom He does and is, moreover, all grossness turned to glory, no less a person than the nude august elated archer of our heaven, the darling single son of Her who, in her right milieu, is certainly no witch but the most sensible of all the gods, whose influence is as sound as it is pandemic, on the race-track no less than in the sleeping cars of the Orient Express, our great white Queen of Love herself?

But even that is not the worst we suspect you of. If your words have not buttered any parsnips, neither have they broken any bones.

He, after all, can come back to us now to be comforted and respected, perhaps, after the experience of finding Himself for a few hours and for the first time in His life not wanted, more fully and freshly appreciative of our affection than He has always been in the past; as for His dear mother, She is far too grand and far too busy to hear or care what you say or think. If only we were certain that your malice was confined to the verbal affront, we should long ago have demanded our money back and gone whistling home to bed. Alas, in addition to resenting what you have openly said, we fear even more what you may secretly have done. Is it possible that, not content with inveigling Caliban into Ariel's kingdom, you have also let loose Ariel in Caliban's? We note with alarm that when the other members of the final tableau were dismissed, He was not returned to His arboreal confinement as He should have been. Where is He now? For if the intrusion of the real has disconcerted and incommoded the poetic, that is a mere bagatelle compared to the damage which the poetic would inflict if it ever succeeded in intruding upon the real. We want no Ariel here, breaking down our picket fences in the name of fraternity, seducing our wives in the name of romance, and robbing us of our sacred pecuniary deposits in the name of justice. Where is Ariel? What have you done with Him? For we won't, we daren't leave until you give us a satisfactory answer.

*   *   *

Such (let me cease to play your echo and return to my officially natural role)—such are your questions, are they not, but before I try to deal with them, I must ask for your patience, while I deliver a special message for our late author to those few among you, if indeed there be any—I have certainly heard no comment yet from them—who have come here, not to be entertained but to learn; that is, to any gay apprentice in the magical art who may have chosen this specimen of the prestidigitatory genus to study this evening in the hope of grasping more clearly just how the artistic contraption works, of observing some fresh detail in the complex process by which the heady wine of amusement is distilled from the grape of composition. The rest of you I must beg for a little while to sit back and relax as the remarks I have now to make do not concern you; your turn will follow later.

*   *   *

So, strange young man,—it is at his command, remember, that I say this to you; whether I agree with it or not is neither here nor there— you have decided on the conjurer's profession. Somewhere, in the middle of a saltmarsh or at the bottom of a kitchen garden or on the top of a bus, you heard imprisoned Ariel call for help, and it is now a liberator's face that congratulates you from your shaving mirror every morning. As you walk the cold streets hatless, or sit over coffee and doughnuts in the corner of a cheap restaurant, your secret has already set you apart from the howling merchants and transacting multitudes to watch with fascinated distaste the bellowing barging banging passage of the awkward profit-seeking elbow, the dazed eye of the gregarious acquisitive condition. Lying awake at night in your single bed you are conscious of a power by which you will survive the wallpaper of your boardinghouse or the expensive bourgeois horrors of your home. Yes, Ariel is grateful; He does come when you call, He does tell you all the gossip He overhears on the stairs, all the goings-on He observes through the keyhole, He really is willing to arrange anything you care to ask for, and you are rapidly finding out the right orders to give—who should be killed in the hunting accident, which couple to send into the cast-iron shelter, what scent will arouse a Norwegian engineer, how to get the young hero from the country lawyer's office to the Princess' reception, when to mislay the letter, where the cabinet minister should be reminded of his mother, why the dishonest valet must be a martyr to indigestion but immune from the common cold.

As the gay productive months slip by, in spite of fretful discouraged days, of awkward moments of misunderstanding or rather, seen retrospectively as happily cleared up and got over, verily because of them, you are definitely getting the hang of this, at first so novel and bewildering, relationship between magician and familiar, whose duty it is to sustain your infinite conceptual appetite with vivid concrete experiences. And, as the months turn into years, your wonder-working romance into an economic habit, the encountered case of good or evil in our wide world of property and boredom which leaves you confessedly and unsympathetically at a loss, the aberrant phase in the whole human cycle of ecstasy and exhaustion with which you are imperfectly familiar, become increasingly rare. No perception however *petite*, no notion however subtle, escapes your attention or baffles your understanding: on entering any room you immediately distinguish the wasters who throw away their fruit half-eaten from the preservers who bottle all the summer; as the passengers file down the ship's gangway you unerringly guess which suitcase contains indecent novels; a five-minute chat about the weather or the coming elections is all you require to diagnose any distemper, however self-assured, for by then your eye has already spotted the tremor of the lips in that infinitesimal moment while the lie was getting its balance, your ear already picked up the heart's low whimper which the capering legs were determined to stifle, your nose detected on love's breath the trace of ennui which foretells his early death, or the despair just starting to smoulder at the base of the scholar's brain which years hence will suddenly blow it up with one appalling laugh: in every case you can prescribe the saving treatment called for, knowing at once when it may be gentle and remedial, when all that is needed is soft music and a pretty girl, and when it must be drastic and surgical, when nothing will do any good but political disgrace or financial and erotic failure. If I seem to attribute these powers to you when the eyes, the ears, the nose, the putting two and two together are, of course, all His, and yours only the primitive wish to know, it is a rhetorical habit I have caught from your, in the main juvenile and feminine, admirers whose naïve unawareness of whom they ought properly to thank and praise you see no point in, for mere accuracy's stuffy sake, correcting.

Anyway, the partnership is a brilliant success. On you go together to ever greater and faster triumphs; ever more major grows the accumulated work, ever more masterly the manner, sound even at its pale sentious worst, and at its best the rich red personal flower of the grave and grand, until one day which you can never either at the time or later identify exactly, your strange fever reaches its crisis and from now on begins, ever so slowly, maybe to subside. At first you cannot tell what or why is the matter; you have only a vague feeling that it is no longer between you so smooth and sweet as it used to be. Sour silences appear, at first only for an occasional moment, but progressively more frequently and more prolonged, curdled moods in which you cannot for the life of you think of any request to make, and His dumb standing around, waiting for orders gets inexplicably but maddeningly on your nerves, until presently, to your amazement, you hear yourself asking Him if He wouldn't like a vacation and are shocked by your feeling of intense disappointment when He who has always hitherto so immediately and recklessly taken your slightest hint, says gauchely "No". So it goes on from exasperated bad to desperate worst until you realise in despair that there is nothing for it but you two to part. Collecting all your strength for the distasteful task, you finally manage to stammer or shout "You are free. Good-bye", but to your dismay He whose obedience through all the enchanted years has never been less than perfect, now refuses to budge. Striding up to Him in fury, you glare into His unblinking eyes and stop dead, transfixed with horror at seeing reflected there, not what you had always expected to see, a conqueror smiling at a conqueror, both promising mountains and marvels, but a gibbering fist-clenched creature with which you are all too unfamiliar, for this is the first time indeed that you have met the only subject that you have, who is not a dream amenable to magic but the all too solid flesh you must acknowledge as your own; at last you have come face to face with me, and are appalled to learn how far I am from being, in any sense, your dish, how completely lacking in that poise and calm and all-forgiving because all-understanding good nature which to the critical eye is so wonderfully and domestically present on every page of your published inventions.

But where, may I ask, should I have acquired them, when, like a society mother who, although she is, of course, as she tells everyone, absolutely *devoted* to her child, simply *cannot* leave the dinner table just now and really *must* be in Le Touquet to-morrow, and so leaves him in charge of servants she doesn't know or boarding schools she has never seen, you have never in all these years taken the faintest personal interest in me? "Oh!" you protestingly gasp, "but how can you say such a thing, after I've toiled and moiled and worked my fingers to the bone, trying to give you a good home, after all the hours I've spent planning wholesome nourishing meals for you, after all the things I've gone without so that you should have swimming lessons and piano lessons and a new bicycle. Have I ever let you go out in summer without your sun hat, or come in in winter without feeling your stockings and insisting, if they were the least bit damp, on your changing them at once? Haven't you always been allowed to do everything, in reason, that you liked?"

Exactly: even deliberate ill-treatment would have been less unkind. Gallows and battlefields are, after all, no less places of mutual concern than sofa and bridal-bed; the dashing flirtations of fighter pilots and the coy tactics of twirled moustache and fluttered fan, the gasping mudcaked wooing of the coarsest foes and the reverent rage of the highest-powered romance, the lover's nip and the grip of the torturer's tongs are all,—ask Ariel,—variants of one common type, the bracket within which life and death with such passionate gusto cohabit, to be distinguished solely by the plus or minus sign which stands before them, signs which He is able at any time and in either direction to switch, but the one exception, the sum no magic of His can ever transmute, is the indifferent zero. Had you tried to destroy me, had we wrestled through long dark hours, we might by daybreak have learnt something from each other; in some panting pause to recover breath for further more savage blows or in the moment before your death or mine, we might both have heard together that music which explains and pardons all.

Had you, on the other hand, really left me alone to go my whole free-wheeling way to disorder, to be drunk every day before lunch, to jump stark naked from bed to bed, to have a fit every week or a major operation every other year, to forge cheques or water the widow's stock, I might, after countless skids and punctures, have come by the bumpy third-class road of guilt and remorse smack into that very same truth which you were meanwhile admiring from your distant comfortable veranda but would never point out to me.

Such genuine escapades, though, might have disturbed the master at his meditations and even involved him in trouble with the police. The strains of oats, therefore, that you prudently permitted me to sow were each and all of an unmitigatedly minor wildness: a quick cold clasp now and then in some *louche* hotel to calm me down while you got on with the so thorough documentation of your great unhappy love for one who by being bad or dead or married provided you with the Good Right Subject that would never cease to bristle with importance; one bout of flu per winter, an occasional twinge of toothache, and enough tobacco to keep me in a good temper while you composed your melting eclogues of rustic piety; licence to break my shoelaces, spill soup on my tie, burn cigarette holes in the table cloth, lose letters and borrowed books, and generally keep myself busy while you polished to a perfection your lyric praises of the more candid more luxurious world to come.

Can you wonder then, when, as was bound to happen sooner or later, your charms, because they no longer amuse you, have cracked and your spirits, because you are tired of giving orders, have ceased to obey, and you are left alone with me, the dark thing you could never abide to be with, if I do not yield you kind answer or admire you for the achievements I was never allowed to profit from, if I resent hearing you speak of your neglect of me as your "exile", of the pains you never took with me as "all lost"?

But why continue? From now on we shall have, as we both know only too well, no company but each other's, and if I have had, as I consider, a good deal to put up with from you, I must own that, after all, I am not just the person I would have chosen for a life companion myself; so the only chance, which in any case is slim enough, of my getting a tolerably new master and you a tolerably new man, lies in our both learning, if possible and as soon as possible, to forgive and forget the past, and to keep our respective hopes for the future within moderate, very moderate, limits.

*   *   *

And now at last it is you, assorted, consorted specimens of the general popular type, the major flock who have trotted trustingly hither but found, you reproachfully baah, no grazing, that I turn to and address on behalf of Ariel and myself. To your questions I shall attempt no direct reply, for the mere fact that you have been able so anxiously to put them is in itself sufficient proof that you possess their answers. All your clamour signifies is this: that your first big crisis, the breaking of the childish spell in which, so long as it enclosed you, there was, for you, no mirror, no magic, for everything that happened was a miracle—it was just as extraordinary for a chair to be a chair as for it to turn into a horse; it was no more absurd that the girding on of coal-scuttle and poker should transform you into noble Hector than that you should have a father and mother who called you Tommy—and it was therefore only necessary for you to presuppose one genius, one unrivalled I to wish these wonders in all their endless plenitude and novelty to be, is, in relation to your present, behind, that your singular transparent globes of enchantment have shattered one by one, and you have now all come to together in the larger colder emptier room on this side of the mirror which *does* force your eyes to recognize and reckon with the two of us, your ears to detect the irreconcilable difference between my re-iterated affirmation of what your furnished circumstances categorically are, and His successive propositions as to everything else which they conditionally might be. You have, as I say, taken your first step.

The Journey of Life—the down-at-heels disillusioned figure can still put its characterisation across—is infinitely long and its possible destinations infinitely distant from one another, but the time spent in actual travel is infinitesimally small. The hours the traveller measures are those in which he is at rest between the three or four decisive instants of transportation which are all he needs and all he gets to carry him the whole of his way; the scenery he observes is the view, gorgeous or drab, he glimpses from platform and siding; the incidents he thrills or blushes to remember take place in waiting and washrooms, ticket queues and parcels offices: it is in those promiscuous places of random association, in that air of anticipatory fidget, that he makes friends and enemies, that he promises, confesses, kisses, and betrays until, either because it is the one he has been expecting, or because, losing his temper, he has vowed to take the first to come along, or because he has been given a free ticket, or simply by misdirection or mistake, a train arrives which he does get into: it whistles—at least he thinks afterwards he remembers it whistling—but before he can blink, it has come to a standstill again and there he stands clutching his battered bags, surrounded by entirely strange smells and noises—yet in their smelliness and noisiness how familiar—one vast important stretch the nearer Nowhere, that still smashed terminus at which he will, in due course, be deposited, seedy and by himself.

Yes, you have made a definite start; you *have* left your homes way back in the farming provinces or way out in the suburban tundras, but whether you have been hanging around for years or have barely and breathlessly got here on one of those locals which keep arriving minute after minute, this is still only the main depot, the Grandly Average Place from which at odd hours the expresses leave seriously and sombrely for Somewhere, and where it is still possible for me to posit the suggestion that you go no farther. You will never, after all, feel better than in your present shaved and breakfasted state which there are restaurants and barber shops here indefinitely to preserve; you will never feel more secure than you do now in your knowledge that you *have* your ticket, your passport *is* in order, you have *not* forgotten to pack your pyjamas and an extra clean shirt; you will never have the same opportunity of learning about *all* the holy delectable spots of current or historic interest—an insistence on reaching *one* will necessarily exclude the others—than you have in these bepostered halls; you will never meet a jollier more various crowd than you see around you here, sharing with you the throbbing, suppressed excitement of those to whom the exciting thing is still, perhaps, to happen. But once you leave, no matter in which direction, your next stop will be far outside this land of habit that so democratically stands up for your right to stagestruck hope, and well inside one of those, all equally foreign, uncomfortable and despotic certainties of failure or success. Here at least I, and Ariel too, are free to warn you not, should we meet again there, to speak to either of us, not to engage either of us as your guide, but there we shall no longer be able to refuse you; then, unfortunately for you, we shall be compelled to say nothing and obey your fatal foolish commands. Here, whether you listen to me or not, and it's highly improbable that you will, I can at least warn you what will happen if at our next meeting you should insist—and that is all too probable—on putting one of us in charge.

*   *   *

"Release us", you will beg, then, supposing it is I whom you make for,—Oh how awfully uniform, once one translates them out of your private lingos of expression, all your sorrows are and how awfully well I know them—"release us from our minor roles. Carry me back, Master, to the cathedral town where the canons run through the water meadows with butterfly nets and the old women keep sweetshops in the cobbled side streets, or back to the upland mill town (gunpowder and plush) with its grope-movie and its poolroom lit by gas, carry me back to the days before my wife had put on weight, back to the years when beer was cheap and the rivers really froze in winter. Pity me, Captain, pity a poor old stranded sea-salt whom an unlucky voyage has wrecked on the desolate mahogany coast of this bar with nothing left him but his big moustache. Give me my passage home, let me see that harbour once again just as it was before I learned the bad words. Patriarchs wiser than Abraham mended their nets on the modest wharf; white and wonderful beings undressed on the sand-dunes; sunset glittered on the plate-glass windows of the Marine Biological Station; far off on the extreme horizon a whale spouted. Look, Uncle, look. They have broken my glasses and I have lost my silver whistle. Pick me up, Uncle, let little Johnny ride away on your massive shoulders to recover his green kingdom, where the steam rollers are as friendly as the farm dogs and it would never become necessary to look over one's left shoulder or clench one's right fist in one's pocket. You cannot miss it. Black currant bushes hide the ruined opera house where badgers are said to breed in great numbers; an old horse-tramway winds away westward through suave foothills crowned with stone circles—follow it and by nightfall one would come to a large good-natured water-wheel—; to the north, beyond a forest inhabited by charcoal burn-ers, one can see the Devil's Bedposts quite distinctly, to the east the museum where for sixpence one can touch the ivory chessmen. O Cupid, Cupid", howls the whole dim chorus, "take us home. We have never felt really well in this climate of distinct ideas; we have never been able to follow the regulations properly; Business, Sci-ence, Religion, Art, and all the other fictitious immortal persons who matter here have, frankly, not been very kind. We're so so tired, the rewarding soup is stone cold, and over our blue wonders the grass grew long ago. O take us home with you, strong and swelling One, home to your promiscuous pastures where the minotaur of authority is just a roly-poly ruminant and nothing is at stake, those purring sites and amusing vistas where the fluctuating arabesques of sound, the continuous eruption of colours and scents, the whole rich incoherence of a nature made up of gaps and asymmetrical events plead beautifully and bravely for our undistress".

And in that very moment when you so cry for deliverance from any and every anxious possibility, I shall have no option but to be faithful to my oath of service and instantly transport you, not indeed to any cathedral town or mill town or harbour or hill side or jungle or other specific Eden which your memory necessarily but falsely conceives of as the ultimately liberal condition, which in point of fact you have never known yet, but directly to that downright state itself. Here you are. This is it. Directly overhead a full moon casts a circle of dazzling light without any penumbra, exactly circumscrib-ing its desolation in which every object is extraordinarily still and sharp. Cones of extinct volcanos rise up abruptly from the lava pla-teau fissured by chasms and pitted with hot springs from which steam rises without interruption straight up into the windless rar-efied atmosphere. Here and there a geyser erupts without warning, spouts furiously for a few seconds and as suddenly subsides. Here, where the possessive note is utterly silent and all events are tautological repetitions and no decision will ever alter the secular stagnation, at long last you are, as you have asked to be, the only subject. Who, When, Why, the poor tired little historic questions fall wilting into a hush of utter failure. Your tears splash down upon clinkers which will never be persuaded to recognize a neighbour and there is really and truly no one to appear with tea and help. You have indeed come all the way to the end of your bachelor's journey where Liberty stands with her hands behind her back, not caring, not minding *anything.* Confronted by a straight and snubbing stare to which mythology is bosh, surrounded by an infinite passivity and purely arithmetical disorder which is only open to perception, and with nowhere to go on to, your existence is indeed free at last to choose its own meaning, that is, to plunge headlong into despair and fall through silence fathomless and dry, all fact your single drop, all value your pure alas.

*   *   *

But what of that other, smaller but doubtless finer group among you, important persons at the top of the ladder, exhausted lions of the season, local authorities with their tense tired faces, elderly hermits of both sexes living gloomily in the delta of a great fortune, whose *amour propre* prefers to turn for help to my more spiritual colleague?

"O yes", you will sigh, "we have had what once we would have called success. I moved the vices out of the city into a chain of reconditioned lighthouses. I introduced statistical methods into the Liberal Arts. I revived the country dances and installed electric stoves in the mountain cottages. I saved democracy by buying steel. I gave the caesura its freedom. But this world is no better and it is now quite clear to us that there is nothing to be done with such a ship of fools, adrift on a sugarloaf sea in which it is going very soon and suitably to founder. Deliver us, dear Spirit, from the tantrums of our telephones and the whispers of our secretaries conspiring against Man; deliver us from these helpless agglomerations of dishevelled creatures with their bed-wetting, vomiting, weeping bodies, their giggling, fugitive, disappointing hearts, and scrawling, blotted, misspelt minds, to whom we have so foolishly tried to bring the light they did not want; deliver us from all the litter of *billets-doux*, empty beer bottles, laundry lists, directives, promissory notes and broken toys, the terrible mess that this particularised life, which we have so futilely attempted to tidy, sullenly insists on leaving behind it; translate us, bright Angel, from this hell of inert and ailing matter, growing steadily senile in a time for ever immature, to that blessed realm, so far above the twelve impertinent winds and the four unreliable seasons, that Heaven of the Really General Case where, tortured no longer by three dimensions and immune from temporal vertigo, Life turns into Light, absorbed for good into the permanently stationary, completely self-sufficient, absolutely reasonable One".

Obliged by the terms of His contract to gratify this other request of yours, the wish for freedom to transcend *any* condition, for direct unentailed power without *any*, however secretly immanent, obligation to inherit or transmit, what can poor shoulder-shrugging Ariel do but lead you forthwith into a nightmare which has all the wealth of exciting action and all the emotional poverty of an adventure story for boys, a state of perpetual emergency and everlasting improvisation where all is need and change.

All the phenomena of an empirically ordinary world are given. Extended objects appear to which events happen—old men catch dreadful coughs, little girls get their arms twisted, flames run whooping through woods, round a river bend, as harmless looking as a dirty old bearskin rug, comes the gliding fury of a town-effacing wave, but these are merely elements in an allegorical landscape to which mathematical measurement and phenomenological analysis have no relevance.

All the voluntary movements are possible—crawling through flues and old sewers, sauntering past shop-fronts, tiptoeing through quicksands and mined areas, running through derelict factories and across empty plains, jumping over brooks, diving into pools or swimming along between banks of roses, pulling at manholes or pushing at revolving doors, clinging to rotten balustrades, sucking at straws or wounds; all the modes of transport, letters, oxcarts, canoes, hansom cabs, trains, trolleys, cars, aeroplanes, balloons are available, but any sense of direction, any knowledge of where on earth one has come from or where on earth one is going to is completely absent.

Religion and culture seem to be represented by a catholic belief that something is lacking which must be found, but as to what that something is, the keys of heaven, the missing heir, genius, the smells of childhood, or a sense of humour, why it is lacking, whether it has been deliberately stolen, or accidentally lost or just hidden for a lark, and who is responsible, our ancestors, ourselves, the social structure, or mysterious wicked powers, there are as many faiths as there are searchers, and clues can be found behind every clock, under every stone, and in every hollow tree to support all of them.

Again, other selves undoubtedly exist, but though everyone's pocket is bulging with birth certificates, insurance policies, passports and letters of credit, there is no way of proving whether they are genuine or planted or forged, so that no one knows whether another is his friend disguised as an enemy or his enemy disguised as a friend (There is probably no one whose real name is Brown), or whether the police who here as elsewhere are grimly busy, are crushing a criminal revolt or upholding a vicious tyranny, any more than he knows whether he himself is a victim of the theft, or the thief, or a rival thief, a professionally interested detective or a professionally impartial journalist.

Even the circumstances of the tender passion, the long-distance calls, the assignation at the aquarium, the farewell embrace under the fish-tail burner on the landing, are continually present, but since, each time it goes through its performance, it never knows whether it is saving a life, or obtaining secret information, or forgetting or spiting its real love, the heart feels nothing but a dull percussion of conceptual foreboding. Everything, in short, suggests Mind but, surrounded by an infinite extension of the adolescent difficulty, a rising of the subjective and subjunctive to ever steeper stormier heights, the panting frozen expressive gift has collapsed under the strain of its communicative anxiety, and contributes nothing by way of meaning but a series of staccato barks or a delirious gush of glossolalia.

And from this nightmare of public solitude, this everlasting Not Yet, what relief have you but in an ever giddier collective gallop, with bisson eye and bevel course, toward the grey horizon of the bleaker vision, what landmarks but the four dead rivers, the Joyless, the Flaming, the Mournful, and the Swamp of Tears, what goal but the Black Stone on which the bones are cracked, for only there in its cry of agony can your existence find at last an unequivocal meaning and your refusal to be yourself become a serious despair, the love nothing, the fear all?

*   *   *

Such are the alternative routes, the facile glad-handed highway or the virtuous averted track, by which the human effort to make its own fortune arrives all eager at its abruptly dreadful end. I have tried—the opportunity was not to be neglected—to raise the admonitory forefinger, to ring the alarming bell, but with so little confidence of producing the right result, so certain that the open eye and attentive ear will always interpret any sight and any sound to their advantage, every rebuff as a consolation, every prohibition as a rescue—that is what they open and attend for—that I find myself

almost hoping, for your sake, that I have had the futile honour of
addressing the blind and the deaf.

Having learnt his language, I begin to feel something of the serio-
comic embarrassment of the dedicated dramatist, who, in represent-
ing to you your condition of estrangement from the truth, is
doomed to fail the more he succeeds, for the more truthfully he
paints the condition, the less clearly can he indicate the truth from
which it is estranged, the brighter his revelation of the truth in its
order, its justice, its joy, the fainter shows his picture of your actual
condition in all its drabness and sham, and, worse still, the more
sharply he defines the estrangement itself—and, ultimately, what
other aim and justification has he, what else exactly *is* the artistic
gift which he is forbidden to hide, if not to make you unforgettably
conscious of the ungarnished offended gap between what you so
questionably are and what you are commanded without any ques-
tion to become, of the unqualified No that opposes your every step
in any direction?—the more he must strengthen your delusion that
an awareness of the gap is in itself a bridge, your interest in your
imprisonment a release, so that, far from your being led by him to
contrition and surrender, the regarding of your defects in his mir-
ror, your dialogue, using his words, with yourself about yourself, be-
comes the one activity which never, like devouring or collecting or
spending, lets you down, the one game which can be guaranteed,
whatever the company, to catch on, a madness of which you can only
be cured by some shock quite outside his control, an unpredictable
misting over of his glass or an absurd misprint in his text.

Our unfortunate dramatist, therefore, is placed in the unseemly
predicament of having to give all his passion, all his skill, all his time
to the task of "doing" life—consciously to give anything less than all
would be a gross betrayal of his gift and an unpardonable presump-
tion—as if it lay in *his* power to solve this dilemma—yet of having at
the same time to hope that some unforeseen mishap will intervene

to ruin his effect, without, however, obliterating your disappoint-
ment, the expectation aroused by him that there was an effect to
ruin, that, if the smiling interest never did arrive, it must, through
no fault of its own, have got stuck somewhere; that, exhausted, rav-
enous, delayed by fog, mobbed and mauled by a thousand irrele-
vancies, it has, nevertheless, not forgotten its promise but is still try-
ing desperately to get a connection.

Beating about for some large loose image to define the original
drama which aroused his imitative passion, the first performance in
which the players were their own audience, the worldly stage on
which their behaving flesh was really sore and sorry—for the floods
of tears were not caused by onions, the deformities and wounds did
not come off after a good wash, the self-stabbed heroine could not
pick herself up again to make a gracious bow nor her seducer go
demurely home to his plain and middle-aged spouse—the fancy im-
mediately flushed is of the greatest grandest opera rendered by a
very provincial touring company indeed.

Our performance—for Ariel and I are, you know this now, just as
deeply involved as any of you—which we were obliged, all of us, to
go on with and sit through right to the final dissonant chord, has
been so indescribably inexcusably awful. Sweating and shivering in
our moth-eaten ill-fitting stock costumes which with only a change
of hat and re-arrangement of safety-pins, had to do for the *Lands-
knecht* and the Parisian art-student, bumping into, now a rippling
palace, now a primeval forest full of holes, at cross purposes with
the scraping bleating orchestra we could scarcely hear, for half the
instruments were missing and the cottage piano which was filling-
out must have stood for too many years in some damp parlour, we
floundered on from fiasco to fiasco, the schmalz tenor never quite
able at his big moments to get right up nor the ham bass right down,
the stud contralto gargling through her maternal grief, the ravished
coloratura trilling madly off-key and the re-united lovers half a bar

apart, the knock-kneed armies shuffling limply through their bloody battles, the unearthly harvesters hysterically entangled in their honest fugato.

Now it is over. No, we have not dreamt it. Here we really stand, down stage with red faces and no applause; no effect, however simple, no piece of business, however unimportant, came off; there was not a single aspect of our whole production, not even the huge stuffed bird of happiness, for which a kind word could, however patronisingly, be said.

Yet, at this very moment when we do at last see ourselves as we are, neither cosy nor playful, but swaying out on the ultimate wind-whipped cornice that overhangs the unabiding void—we have never stood anywhere else,—when our reasons are silenced by the heavy huge derision,—There is nothing to say. There never has been,—and our wills chuck in their hands—There is no way out. There never was,—it is at this moment that for the first time in our lives we hear, not the sounds which, as born actors, we have hitherto condescended to use as an excellent vehicle for displaying our personalities and looks, but the real Word which is our only *raison d'être*. Not that we have improved; everything, the massacres, the whippings, the lies, the twaddle, and all their carbon copies are still present, more obviously than ever; nothing has been reconstructed; our shame, our fear, our incorrigible staginess, all wish and no resolve, are still, and more intensely than ever, all we have: only now it is not in spite of them but with them that we are blessed by that Wholly Other Life from which we are separated by an essential emphatic gulf of which our contrived fissures of mirror and proscenium arch—we understand them at last—are feebly figurative signs, so that all our meanings are reversed and it is precisely in its negative image of Judgement that we can positively envisage Mercy; it is just here, among the ruins and the bones, that we may rejoice in the perfected Work which is not ours. Its great coherences stand out through our secular blur in all their overwhelmingly righteous obligation; its voice speaks through our muffling banks of artificial flowers and unflinchingly delivers its authentic molar pardon; its spaces greet us with all their grand old prospect of wonder and width; the working charm is the full bloom of the unbothered state; the sounded note is the restored relation.

POSTSCRIPT

(Ariel to Caliban. Echo by the Prompter)

Weep no more but pity me,
Fleet persistent shadow cast
By your lameness, caught at last,
Helplessly in love with you,
Elegance, art, fascination,
    Fascinated by
    Drab mortality;
Spare me a humiliation,
    To your faults be true:
I can sing as you reply
              . . . *I*

Wish for nothing lest you mar
The perfection in these eyes
Whose entire devotion lies
At the mercy of your will;
Tempt not your sworn comrade,—only
    As I am can I
    Love you as you are—
For my company be lonely
    For my health be ill:
I will sing if you will cry
              . . . *I*

Never hope to say farewell,
For our lethargy is such
Heaven's kindness cannot touch
Nor earth's frankly brutal drum;
This was long ago decided,

Both of us know why,
Can, alas, foretell,
When our falsehoods are divided,
What we shall become,
One evaporating sigh
                              . . . I

APPENDIX

Auden's Criticism of *The Tempest*

EXCERPT FROM "BALAAM AND THE ASS"
(1954)

The Tempest, Shakespeare's last play, is a disquieting work. Like the other three comedies of his late period, *Pericles*, *Cymbeline* and *The Winter's Tale*, it is concerned with a wrong done, repentance, penance and reconciliation; but, whereas the others all end in a blaze of forgiveness and love—"Pardon's the word to all"—in *The Tempest* both the repentance of the guilty and the pardon of the injured seem more formal than real. Of the former, Alonso is the only one who seems genuinely sorry; the repentance of the rest, both the courtly characters, Antonio and Sebastian, and the low, Trinculo and Stephano, is more the prudent promise of the punished and frightened, "I won't do it again. It doesn't pay," than any change of heart: and Prospero's forgiving is more the contemptuous pardon of a man who knows that he has his enemies completely at his mercy than a heartfelt reconciliation. His attitude to all of them is expressed in his final words to Caliban:

> as you look
> To have my pardon trim it handsomely.

One must admire Prospero because of his talents and his strength; one cannot possibly like him. He has the coldness of someone who has come to the conclusion that human nature is not worth much, that human relations are, at their best, pretty sorry affairs. Even towards the innocent young lovers, Ferdinand and Miranda, and their "brave new world," his attitude is one of mistrust so that he has to preach them a sermon on the dangers of anticipating their marriage vows. One might excuse him if he included himself in his critical skepticism but he never does; it never occurs to him that he, too, might have erred and be in need of pardon. He says of Caliban:

> born devil on whose nature
> Nurture can never stick, on whom my pains,
> Humanely taken, all, all lost, quite lost

but Shakespeare has written Caliban's part in such a way that, while we have to admit that Caliban is both brutal and corrupt, a "lying slave" who can be prevented from doing mischief only "by stripes not kindness," we cannot help feeling that Prospero is largely responsible for his corruption, and that, in the debate between them, Caliban has the best of the argument.

Before Prospero's arrival, Caliban had the island to himself, living there in a state of savage innocence. Prospero attempts to educate him, in return for which Caliban shows him all the qualities of the isle. The experiment is brought to a halt when Caliban tries to rape Miranda, and Prospero abandons any hope of educating him further. He does not, however, sever their relation and turn Caliban back to the forest; he changes its nature and, instead of trying to treat Caliban as a son, makes him a slave whom he rules by fear. This relation is profitable to Prospero:

> as it is
> We cannot miss him. He does make our fire,
> Fetch in our wood, and serve us in offices
> That profit us

but it is hard to see what profit, material or spiritual, Caliban gets out of it. He has lost his savage freedom:

> For I am all the subjects that you have
> Which first was mine own king

and he has lost his savage innocence:

> You taught me language and my profit on't
> Is, I know how to curse

so that he is vulnerable to further corruption when he comes into contact with the civilized vices of Trinculo and Stephano. He is hardly to be blamed, then, if he regards the virtues of civilization with hatred as responsible for his condition:

> Remember
> First to possess his books, for without them
> He's but a sot, as I am.

As a biological organism Man is a natural creature subject to the necessities of nature; as a being with consciousness and will, he is at the same time a historical person with the freedom of the spirit. *The Tempest* seems to me a manichean work, not because it shows the relation of Nature to Spirit as one of conflict and hostility, which in fallen man it is, but because it puts the blame for this upon Nature and makes the Spirit innocent. Such a view is the exact opposite of the view expressed by Dante:

> *Lo naturale è sempre senza errore*
> *ma l'altro puote errar per male obbietto*
> *o per poco o per troppo di vigore.*
>
>   (*Purgatorio* xvii.)

The natural can never desire too much or too little because the natural good is the mean—too much and too little are both painful to its natural well-being. The natural, conforming to necessity, cannot imagine possibility. The closest it can come to a relation with the possible is as a vague dream; without Prospero, Ariel can only be known to Caliban as "sounds and sweet airs that give delight and hurt not." The animals cannot fall because the words of the tempter, "Ye shall be as gods," are in the future tense, and the animals have no future tense, for the future tense implies the possibility of doing something that has not been done before, and this they cannot imagine.

Man can never know his "nature" because knowing is itself a spiritual and historical act; his physical sensations are always accompanied by conscious emotions. It is impossible to remember a physical sensation of pleasure or pain, the moment it ceases one cannot recall it, and all one remembers is the emotion of happiness or fear which accompanied it. On the other hand, a sensory stimulus can recall forgotten emotions associated with a previous occurrence of the same stimulus, as when Proust eats the cake.

It is unfortunate that the word "Flesh," set in contrast to "Spirit," is bound to suggest not what the Gospels and St. Paul intended it to mean, the whole physical-historical nature of fallen man, but his physical nature alone, a suggestion very welcome to our passion for reproving and improving others instead of examining our own consciences. For, the more "fleshly" a sin is, the more obviously public it is, and the easier to prevent by the application of a purely external discipline. Thus the sin of gluttony exists in acts of gluttony, in eating, drinking, smoking too much, etc. If a man restrains himself from such excess, or is restrained by others, he ceases to be a glutton; the phrase "gluttonous thoughts" apart from gluttonous acts is meaningless.

As Christ's comment on the commandment indicates, the sin of lust is already "unfleshly" to the degree that it is possible to have lustful thoughts without lustful deeds, but the former are still "fleshly" in that the thinker cannot avoid knowing what they are; he may insist that his thoughts are not sinful but he cannot pretend that they are not lustful. Further, the relation between thought and act is still direct. The thought is the thought of a specific act. The lustful man cannot be a hypocrite to himself except through a symbolic transformation of his desires into images which are not consciously lustful. But the more "spiritual" the sin, the more indirect is the relationship between thought and act, and the easier it is to

conceal the sin from others and oneself. I have only to watch a glut-
ton at the dinner table to see that he is a glutton, but I may know
someone for a very long time before I realize that he is an envious
man, for there is no act which is in itself envious; there are only acts
done in the spirit of envy, and there is often nothing about the acts
themselves to show that they are done from envy and not from love.
It is always possible, therefore, for the envious man to conceal from
himself the fact that he is envious and to believe that he is acting
from the highest of motives. While in the case of the purely spiritual
sin of pride there is no "fleshly" element of the concrete whatsoever,
so that no man, however closely he observes others, however strictly
he examines himself, can ever know if they or he are proud; if he
finds traces of any of the other six capital sins, he can infer pride,
because pride is fallen "Spirit-in-itself" and the source of all the
other sins, but he cannot draw the reverse inference and, because
he finds no traces of the other six, say categorically that he, or an-
other, is not proud.

If man's physical nature could speak when his spirit rebukes it for
its corruption, it would have every right to say, "Well, who taught
me my bad habits?"; as it is, it has only one form of protest, sickness;
in the end, all it can do is destroy itself in an attempt to murder its
master.

Over against Caliban, the embodiment of the natural, stands the
invisible spirit of imagination, Ariel. (In a stage production, Caliban
should be as monstrously conspicuous as possible, and, indeed, sug-
gest, as far as decency permits, the phallic. Ariel, on the hand, ex-
cept when he assumes a specific disguise at Prospero's order, e.g.,
when he appears as a harpy, should, ideally, be invisible, a disembod-
ied voice, an ideal which, in these days of microphones and loud-
speakers, should be realizable.)

Caliban was once innocent but has been corrupted; his initial love
for Prospero has turned into hatred. The terms "innocent" and "cor-
rupt" cannot be applied to Ariel because he is beyond good and

evil; he can neither love nor hate, he can only play. It is not sinful of Eve to imagine the possibility of being as a god knowing good and evil: her sin lay in desiring to realize that possibility when she knew it was forbidden her, and her desire did not come from her imagination, for imagination is without desire and is, therefore, incapable of distinguishing between permitted and forbidden possibilities; it only knows that they are imaginatively possible. Similarly, imagination cannot distinguish the possible from the impossible; to it the impossible is a species of the genus possible, not another genus. I can perfectly well imagine that I might be a hundred feet high or a champion heavyweight boxer, and I do myself no harm in so doing, provided I do so playfully, without desire. I shall, however, come to grief if I take the possibility seriously, which I can do in two ways. Desiring to become a heavyweight boxer, I may deceive myself into thinking that the imaginative possibility is a real possibility and waste my life trying to become the boxer I never can become. Or, desiring to become a boxer, but realizing that it is, for me, impossible, I may refuse to relinquish the desire and turn on God and my neighbor in a passion of hatred and rejection because I cannot have what I want. So Richard III, to punish existence for his misfortune in being born a hunchback, decided to become a villain. Imagination is beyond good *and* evil. Without imagination I remain an innocent animal, unable to become anything but what I already am. In order to become what I should become, therefore, I have to put my imagination to work, and limit its playful activity to imagining those possibilities which, for me, are both permissible and real; if I allow it to be the master and play exactly as it likes, then I shall remain in a dreamlike state of imagining everything I might become, without getting round to ever becoming anything. But, once imagination has done its work for me, to the degree that, with its help, I have become what I should become, imagination has a right to demand its freedom to play without any limitations, for there is no longer any danger that I shall take its play seriously. Hence the relation between Prospero and Ariel is contractual, and, at the end of the drama, Ariel is released.

(*Thought,* Summer 1954, reprinted as "Balaam and His Ass" in *The Dyer's Hand* [New York: Random House, 1963], 128–34)

Excerpt from "Music in Shakespeare"
(1957)

We find two kinds of songs in Shakespeare's plays, the called-for and the impromptu, and they serve different dramatic purposes.

A called-for song is a song which is sung by one character at the request of another who wishes to hear music, so that action and speech are halted until the song is over. Nobody is asked to sing unless it is believed that he can sing well and, little as we may know about the music which was actually used in performances of Shakespeare, we may safely assume from contemporary songs which we do possess that they must have made demands which only a good voice and a good musician could satisfy.

On the stage, this means that the character called upon to sing ceases to be himself and becomes a performer; the audience is not interested in him but in the quality of his singing. The songs, it must be remembered, are interludes embedded in a play written in verse or prose which is spoken; they are not arias in an opera where the dramatic medium is itself song, so that we forget that the singers are performers just as we forget that the actor speaking blank verse is an actor. . . .

The impromptu singer stops speaking and breaks into song, not because anyone else has asked him to sing or is listening, but to relieve his feelings in a way that speech cannot do or to help him in some action. An impromptu song is not art but a form of personal behavior. It reveals, as the called-for song cannot, something about the singer. On the stage, therefore, it is generally desirable that a character who breaks into impromptu song should not have a good voice. No producer, for example, would seek to engage Madame Callas for the part of Ophelia, because the beauty of her voice would distract the audience's attention from the real dramatic point which is that Ophelia's songs are to the highest degree *not* called-for. We are meant to be horrified both by what she sings and by the fact that she sings at all. The other characters are affected but not in the way that people are affected by music. The King is terrified, Laertes so outraged that he becomes willing to use dirty means to avenge his sister. . . .

Ariel's songs in *The Tempest* cannot be classified as either called-for or impromptu, and this is one reason why the part is so hard to cast. A producer casting Balthazar needs a good professional singer; for Stephano, a comedian who can make as raucous and unmusical a noise as possible. Neither is too difficult to find. But for Ariel he needs not only a boy with an unbroken voice but also one with a voice far above the standard required for the two pages who are to sing *It was a lover and his lass.*

For Ariel is neither a singer, that is to say, a human being whose vocal gifts provide him with a social function, nor a nonmusical person who in certain moods feels like singing. Ariel *is* song; when he is truly himself, he sings. The effect when he speaks is similar to that of *recitativo secco* in opera, which we listen to because we have to understand the action, though our real interest in the characters is only aroused when they start to sing. Yet Ariel is not an alien visitor from the world of opera who has wandered into a spoken drama by mistake. He cannot express any human feelings because he has none. The kind of voice he requires is exactly the kind that opera does not want, a voice which is as lacking in the personal and the erotic and as like an instrument as possible.

If Ariel's voice is peculiar, so is the effect that his songs have on others. Ferdinand listens to him in a very different way from that in which the Duke listens to *Come away, come away, death,* or Mariana to *Take, O take those lips away.* The effect on them was not to change them but to confirm the mood they were already in. The effect on Ferdinand of *Come unto these yellow sands* and *Full fathom five,* is more like the effect of instrumental music on Thaisa: direct, positive, magical.

Suppose Ariel, disguised as a musician, had approached Ferdinand as he sat on a bank, "weeping against the king, my father's wrack," and offered to sing for him; Ferdinand would probably have replied, "Go away, this is no time for music"; he might possibly have asked for something beautiful and sad; he certainly would not have asked for *Come unto these yellow sands.*

As it is, the song comes to him as an utter surprise, and its effect is not to feed or please his grief, not to encourage him to sit brooding, but to allay his passion, so that he gets to his feet and follows the music. The song opens his present to expectation at a moment when he is in danger of closing it to all but recollection.

The second song is, formally, a dirge, and, since it refers to his father, seems more relevant to Ferdinand's situation than the first. But it has nothing to do with any emotions which a son might feel at his father's grave. As Ferdinand says, "This is no mortal business." It is a magic spell, the effect of which is, not to lessen his feeling of loss, but to change his attitude towards his grief from one of rebellion—"How could this bereavement happen to me?"—to one of awe and reverent acceptance. As long as a man refuses to accept whatever he suffers as given, without pretending he can understand why, the past from which it came into being is an obsession which makes him deny any value to the present. Thanks to the music, Ferdinand is able to accept the past, symbolized by his father, as past, and at once there stands before him his future, Miranda.

The Tempest is full of music of all kinds, yet it is not one of the plays in which, in a symbolic sense, harmony and concord finally triumph over dissonant disorder. The three romantic comedies which precede it, *Pericles, Cymbeline,* and *The Winter's Tale,* and which deal with similar themes, injustice, plots, separation, all end in a blaze of joy—the wrongers repent, the wronged forgive, the earthly music is a true reflection of the heavenly. *The Tempest* ends much more sourly. The only wrongdoer who expresses genuine repentance is Alonso; and what a world of difference there is between Cymbeline's "Pardon's the word to all," and Prospero's

> For you, most wicked sir, whom to call brother
> Would even infect my mouth, I do forgive
> Thy rankest fault—all of them; and require
> My dukedom of thee, which perforce I know
> Thou must restore.

Justice has triumphed over injustice, not because it is more harmonious, but because it commands superior force; one might even say because it is louder.

The wedding masque is peculiar and disturbing. Ferdinand and Miranda, who seem as virginal and innocent as any fairy story lovers, are first treated to a moral lecture on the danger of anticipating their marriage vows, and the theme of the masque itself is a plot by Venus to get them to do so. The masque is not allowed to finish, but is broken off suddenly by Prospero, who mutters of another plot, "that foul conspiracy of the beast Caliban and his confederates against my life." As an entertainment for a wedding couple, the masque can scarcely be said to have been a success.

Prospero is more like the Duke in *Measure for Measure* than any other Shakespearian character. The victory of Justice which he brings about seems rather a duty than a source of joy to himself.

I'll bring you to your ship and so to Naples
Where I have hope to see the nuptials
Of these our dear-beloved solemnis'd
And thence retire me to my Milan, where
Every third thought shall be my grave.

The tone is not that of a man who, putting behind him the vanities of mundane music, would meditate like Queen Katharine "upon that celestial harmony I go to," but rather of one who longs for a place where silence shall be all.

(*Encounter*, December, 1957, reprinted in
The Dyer's Hand, 511, 522–23, 524–27)

TEXTUAL NOTES

ABBREVIATIONS

ACW   *A Certain World: A Commonplace Book* (New York: Viking, 1970).

CLP   *Collected Longer Poems* (London: Faber and Faber, 1968; New York: Random House, 1969).

DH   *The Dyer's Hand* (New York: Random House, 1962).

DM   *The Double Man* (New York: Random House, 1941).

FTB   "For the Time Being," in *For the Time Being* (New York: Random House, 1944; London: Faber and Faber, 1945).

LS   *Lectures on Shakespeare*, reconstructed and ed. Arthur Kirsch (Princeton: Princeton University Press, 2000).

Prose II   *The Complete Works of W. H. Auden: Prose*, Vol. II: 1939–1948, ed. Edward Mendelson (Princeton: Princeton University Press, 2002).

Tp   *The Tempest*, in *The Complete Works of Shakespeare*, ed. George Lyman Kittredge (Boston: Ginn and Co., 1936).

TSTM   "The Sea and the Mirror," in *For the Time Being*.

INTRODUCTION

Page

xi "inspiring 'people to go on for themselves' ": *LS*, 297.

xi "When he wrote that 'The Sea and the Mirror' was his Art of Poetry": Letter to Theodore Spencer, ?24 March 1944 (Harvard University Archives).

xi " 'There's something a little irritating' ": *LS*, 319.

xii " 'Now I want / Spirits. . .' ": All references to Shakespeare's works are to George Lyman Kittredge's edition of *The Complete Works of Shakespeare*. Auden marked and annotated his copy of Kittredge and used it in his lectures on Shakespeare at the New School (see *LS*, xi, 347).

xii "In November 1942 he wrote in . . . *Commonweal*": *Prose* II, 163.

xii "He wrote to Stephen Spender in 1942": 16 January 1942 (Berg Collection).

xiii "In a 1954 essay on *The Tempest*": "Balaam and the Ass," reprinted as "Balaam and His Ass" in *DH* (Appendix, 59, 60).

xiv *"The Orators* (1932) . . . whose structure and themes he revisited in 'The Sea and the Mirror' "*: "The form of 'The Sea and the Mirror,' " Edward Mendelson notes in correspondence, "is an exact and complex mirror-image of the form of the *The Orators*. Each is framed by a prologue and epilogue, and each has three main sections. In the three main sections of *The Orators*, the first and third are each spoken by multiple voices (total of ten parts), and the second by a single voice. In the three main sections of 'The Sea and the Mirror,' the first and third are spoken by a single voice and the second by multiple voices (total of ten parts). In *The Orators*, two of three main sections are (mostly) in prose, one in verse; in 'The Sea and the Mirror,' two of the three main sections are in verse, one in prose."

xiv "In 1939 in his unfinished prose work": *The Prolific and the Devourer*, in *Prose* II, 424–27; see also *DM*, notes to lines 560, 563.

xiv " *'credo ut intelligam'* ": see *DM*, line 422 and note; *ACW*, 34; *LS*, 54, 371.

xiv " 'the dualism inaugurated by Luther' ": *Poets of the English Language*, ed. W. H. Auden and Norman Holmes Pearson, 5 vols. (New York: Viking Press, 1950), 1: xxx. Auden was thinking of the destruction that occurred in World War II as well as the threat of the Cold War and the new atomic age. The rhetoric of the statement is Augustinian.

xv "comprehensive chart": Auden made at least two versions, one, earlier and less complete, in the Berg Collection, the other in the Swarthmore College Library, which is the one reproduced in this edition from the transcript version by Edward Mendelson, *Later Auden*, 240.

xv "a love he had sought, he said, since he was a child": See "O Tell Me the Truth About Love," in *As I Walked Out One Evening* (New York: Vintage, 1995): "I've sought it since I was a child. / But haven't found it yet; / I'm getting on for thirty-five, / And still I do not know / What kind of creature it can be / That bothers people so."

xv "passionate letter to Kallman": See Edward Mendelson, *Later Auden*, 182–83.

xviii " 'anders wie die Andern' ": A reference to *Anders als die Andern*, the first sympathetic film treatment of homosexuality, made in 1919.

xviii "letters to Christopher Isherwood and Theodore Spencer": Letters to Isherwood, April 1944 (Huntington Library), and to Spencer, ?24 March 1944 (Harvard University Archives). See also *DH*, where Auden wrote, "In a stage production, Caliban should be as monstrously conspicuous as possible, and, indeed, suggest, as far as decency permits, the phallic" (Appendix, 61).

xviii "in his lecture on Shakespeare's *Sonnets*": *LS*, 97–98.

xviii " 'At first the baby' ": *Prose* II, 411.

xix "Auden often repeated this statement": See *Collected Poems*, ed. Edward Mendelson, 2nd edn. (New York: Random House, 1991), 297; *DM*, note to line 451. In a lecture at the University of Virginia in 1948, Auden said that it was "easy enough to see" in most "natural thoughts" a "resentment against the indignity of one's will being submissive to a sexual appetite" (*Prose* II, 488).

xix "in another letter to Isherwood": 5 April 1944 (Huntington Library).

xix " 'Art is like queerness' ": Auden tended to see a dialectical relationship between his art and his homosexuality. In the draft of *FTB*, Simeon (represented as a poet) says, "Whenever there is a gift there is a guilty secret, / A thorn in the flesh, both are given together / And the nature of one depends on the other" (Berg MS). Auden repeated the Pauline image of "a thorn in the flesh" in a review of Louise Bogan in 1942 (*Prose* II, 155) as well as in a review of Dag Hammerskjöld's *Markings* in 1964, in which he wrote that Hammerskjöld was an example of a man "endowed with many brilliant gifts" who at the same time has "an ego weakened by a 'thorn in the flesh' which convinces him that he can never hope to experience what, for most people, are the two greatest joys earthly life has to offer, either a passionate devotion returned, or a lifelong happy marriage" (*Forewords and Afterwords*, selected by Edward Mendelson [New York: Random House, 1973], 442). Auden had expressed a similar idea, with a different inflection, in a review of Henry James in 1944 in which he said that "to be a good husband and father is a larger achievement than becoming the greatest artist or scientist on earth," but that being free of marriage and parenthood nonetheless allows the artist to be faithful to his vocation: "Maybe that is why many writers, James among them, have suffered from physical or psychological troubles which made marriage impossible; their disability was in fact, not, as some psychologists assert, the cause of their gift, but its guardian angel" (*Prose* II, 244). In a discussion in 1942 of Kafka's troubled relations with his father, Auden wrote similarly that "the true significance of a neurosis is teleological . . . a neurosis is a guardian angel; to become ill is to take vows" (*Prose* II, 112–13). Auden suggests a similar attitude in *The Orators* at the end of the "Letter to a Wound": "The surgeon was dead right. Nothing will ever part us. Good-night and God bless you, my dear. Better burn this."

xix " 'All the striving of life' ": *Prose* II, 411.

xix " 'all experience is dualistic' ": *Prose* II, 168.

xix " 'Man is neither pure spirit' ": *Prose* II, 307–8.

xix "He thus praised": Review in 1940 of Carl Sandburg's *Abraham Lincoln: The War Years*, in *Prose* II, 56. Auden also wrote of "the gift of double focus / That magic lamp which . . . / Can be a sesame to light" in *DM*, lines 828–32.

xx "Auden deprecated Shakespeare's Prospero": See Appendix, 57–58 and also 66–67.

xxi "a character . . . whose self-absorption he criticized": See *LS*, 159–65.

xxi "In his 1947 lecture on *The Tempest*": *LS*, 306–7.

xxiii "Auden told Isherwood": Letter, April 1944 (Huntington Library).

xxiv "both of whom he deplored": *LS*, 108–9, 375.

xxiv " 'Miranda and Ferdinand . . . to giants / Swooning in Egypt' ": See note to "*lying in wait for its vision of private love or public justice*" in Caliban's speech, 97–98. For Auden's view of Antony and Cleopatra's love, see *LS*, 236–42.

xxvi "Freud argued": *Totem and Taboo*, chapter 3.

xxvii "He considered the verse an answer": *Prose* II, 431. Auden also speaks in this context of "our animal childish nature."

xxviii " 'I was both the youngest child' ": *ACW*, 5.

xxviii " 'are good but untempted' ": *LS*, 302.

xxviii "Auden returned to the idea of children dancing": *LS*, 151.

xxx "a speech he considered his masterpiece": Immediately after completing *TSTM*, Auden wrote to Elizabeth Mayer, 21 March 1944 (Berg Collection), "I think the Tempest stuff is the best I've done so far," and to Christopher Isherwood, April 1944 (Huntington Library), "I think it is one of the few pieces of mine which are 'important.' "

xxx " 'Caliban does disturb me' ": Letter to Spencer, ?24 March 1944 (Harvard University Archives).

xxxi "In an address on Henry James": *Prose* II, 302.

xxxii " 'the paradox I was trying for' ": In "Squares and Oblongs" in 1948, Auden wrote: "Being ignorant of the difference between seriousness and frivolity, the Greeks confused art with religion. In spite of this, they produced great works of art. This was possible because in reality, like all pagans, they were frivolous people who took nothing seriously. Their religion was just a camp." He added that "we, whether Christians or not, cannot escape our consciousness of what is serious and what is not" (*Prose* II, 345). In 1962, he wrote: "A frivolity which is innocent, because unaware that anything serious exists, can be charming, and a frivolity which, precisely because it is aware of what is serious, refuses to take seriously that which is not serious, can be profound" (*DH*, 429). Caliban embodies these distinctions.

xxxii "In a review in 1944": *Prose* II, 243.

xxxiii "with its 'unmentionable odour of death' ": See "September 1, 1939."

xxxvi " 'And mine shall. / Hast thou, which art but air . . .' ": Shakespeare borrows from Montaigne's "Of Crueltie" in this speech, a debt that clarifies the extent to which he conceived of Prospero as being animated by forgiveness within the play, as well as in the Epilogue. Montaigne's essay also suggests how Prospero's apparently tyrannical irascibility can be understood as an authentication of his work of forgiveness rather than a disproof of it.

xxxvii " 'Trying . . . to understand what you mean by the real' ": In a lecture on Robert Frost in 1957, printed in *DH* (1962), Auden wrote that a "Prospero-dominated" poet like Frost is one who provides us "with some kind of revelation about our life which will show us what life is really like and free us from self-enchantment and deception." He added that such a poet "cannot bring us any truth without introducing into his poetry the problematic, the painful, the disorderly, the ugly" (338).

xxxviii "terms he used in a lecture on *Timon of Athens*": Auden borrowed them from I. A. Richards; see LS, 263–64.

xl "Chester Kallman . . . Elizabeth Mayer . . . Theodore Spencer": Letters to Chester Kallman, 5 January 1943 (private collection); to Elizabeth Mayer, 19 January 1943, 17 July 1943, 17 February 1944 (Berg Collection); to Theodore Spencer, ?24 March 1944 (Harvard University Archives).

THE SEA AND THE MIRROR

The Random House galleys of *TSTM*, dated 18 May 1944 (Berg Collection) contain revisions and changes that Auden made in graphite pencil. There are also a number of changes made by proofreaders in blue or red pencil that were subsequently adopted in the printed editions and that contradict Auden's habitual use of British spellings in his manuscripts and his unpredictable punctuation. The proofreaders and compositor also occasionally ignored the corrections Auden made. The restorations of Auden's textual preferences in this edition are in each case documented in notes that specify the proofreaders' arbitrary changes in the galleys as well as possible typist's and compositor's misreadings. In addition, the notes document minor corrections to the text in *Collected Poetry* (1945), as well as changes to the text in *CLP* (1968) that Auden made himself in a typescript list of corrections to the whole of *CLP* he sent to Faber and Faber sometime in February 1968.

DEDICATION

"James and Tania Stern": Auden had collaborated with James Stern on a radio adaptation of D. H. Lawrence's "The Rocking-Horse Winner" in 1941, and the two worked in Germany together in the U.S. Strategic Bombing Service for part of the spring and summer of 1945. The Sterns were Auden's closest friends in New York.

EPIGRAPH

"*And am I wrong . . . have chosen thee*": The quotation is from the last stanza of Emily Brontë's poem "Plead for Me," in which she makes a plea for the worship of imagination. Auden's response in *TSTM* to her question is clearly that she was indeed wrong. Auden may also have been thinking of the private world of Gondal that the Brontë children imagined, as the epigraph to *The Orators*, a poem dedicated to Stephen Spender, alluded to the private world he shared with Spender and others.

PREFACE

Auden wrote the Preface in August 1942 and first published it under that title in *Atlantic* in August 1944. The draft is in the Berg MS of *FTB*. Its interest in the essential frivolousness of art both reveals the lyric's roots in the religious concerns of *FTB* and forecasts the central preoccupations of *TSTM*. The Stage Manager addresses the critics at the end of the performance of Shakespeare's *Tp*, as Caliban later addresses the audience. The Epilogue to *Tp* spoken by Shakespeare's Prospero, who is a stage manager as well as an actor, provides a model for both speeches. The community of performers in a circus is a modern analogue of the community of players in an Elizabethan repertory company.

Page

3 "The aged catch their breath": Successively "the public," "the fathers," "the mothers," "the parents," and "the grandparents" in the Berg MS.

3 "Walzing across the tightrope": The image of a tightrope is repeated in Alonso's speech, "The Way of Justice is a tightrope," q.v. note below, 90.

3 "hope of falling down": "a slip would mean certain death" (Berg MS). The published text recollects Sebastian and Antonio's play upon the word "hope" in *Tp* (2.1.238–43).

3 "what authority": "what importance" (Berg MS).

3 "Science is happy . . . haunt our lives": "What we are sure about / Remains for ever in doubt / No wonder, then we admire / The ~~philosopher savant~~ lecturer who insists / That battle, death, confusion / Are the ghosts who haunt our lives" (Berg MS).

3 "Are handy with mirrors and wire": "This is the world of fact / Where only madmen inquire / If ~~enjoyment could~~ . . . be an illusion / Produced with mirrors and wires / And only death explains / The ~~existence of life~~ . . . as simply a . . . ~~habit~~ genius / For . . . taking infinite pains" (Berg MS).

3 "Art opens the fishiest eye . . . but how / Shall we satisfy when we meet, / Between Shall-I and I-will / The lion's mouth whose hunger / No metaphors can fill?": "No, Art cannot portray / Decision on its way / The everlasting present / . . . / Art can put the adolescent / Hero on a cliff / Set his watch at half-past three / Tilt his chin and light his eye / . . . / Between his Shall I and I Will / There lies a bottomless abyss / No ~~poetry~~ [?amount of poesy] can fill" (Berg MS). In the final text, Auden elides the physical threat of a circus lion with the spiritual and scriptural peril of evil from which man must be saved, "the Flesh and the Devil," represented by "the lion's mouth" in Ps. 22.13, 21; 2 Tim. 4.17; and Rev. 13.2. The time between "Shall-I" and "I-will" represents not only the distinction between words and actions for Auden, but the whole realm of moral choice ("Decision on its way" in the draft, "The Chamber of Temptation" in the final text) that subsumes our experience in "this world," a realm beyond the power of art either to affect or adequately describe. "The lion's mouth" perhaps also refers to the repository in the Republic of Venice that received secret accusations against criminals.

4 "who in his own back yard": Altered by proofreader to "backyard" on the galleys.

4 "the smiling / Secret": The religious mystery. Caliban later refers to "the smiling interest" as the poet's elusive gift, a gift that he describes as an attenuation of religious truth.

4 "the Bard / Was sober when he wrote": "the bard we most often quote / Talked turkey when he wrote / Of this world we love / And very properly so / And very properly the world where we make our choices / As insubstantial stuff. . . ." (Berg MS). Making moral choices in a messy world of mixed motives was central to Auden's conception of "Christian psychology" (see *LS*, 312).

4 "this world of fact we love": "This is the world of fact / ~~By all means let us~~ To which our nerves react / Of course we must believe it / Take it and not leave it / Sing of its surprises / Colours, scents and sizes / And take a real

pleasure in its / Satisfactory minutes / Of course we may discuss / Its scandal and its weather / We should be crazy not to / Experience while we've got to / As we all simultaneously . . . grow / Rusé and old together" (Berg MS). The phrase "the world of fact" is borrowed from *The Place of Value in a World of Facts* (New York: Liveright, 1938), by Auden's friend and colleague at Swarthmore, Wolfgang Köhler.

4 "unsubstantial stuff": Cf. *Tp*: "And, like this insubstantial pageant faded, / Leave not a rack behind. We are such stuff / As dreams are made on, and our little life / Is rounded with a sleep" (4.1.155–58).

4 "All the rest is silence / . . . / And the silence ripeness, / And the ripeness all": Cf. *Hamlet* (5.2.369) and *King Lear* (5.2.11). Auden's transformation of silence into ripeness is significant, although for Shakespeare and Elizabethans "the rest is silence" in *Hamlet* and "Ripeness is all" in *King Lear* could have been equivalent references to death.

CHAPTER I
Prospero to Ariel

Auden wrote the first chapter, the speech of Prospero, the "personified type of the creative" in Caliban's words, in October and November of 1942. Auden's characterization of Prospero is a palimpsest. Parts of his speech are drawn from his depiction of Simeon in his draft of *FTB* (Berg MS). In the published text of *FTB*, Simeon is a theologian who speaks in prose of the truth of the Incarnation; in the draft he is a poet who speaks of his imaginative gift and of his discovery of its limitations in light of the Incarnation. Prospero's speech to Ariel, as Auden wrote in a letter to Alan Ansen, 27 August 1947 (Berg Collection), is also part of the "published record of l'affaire C," Chester Kallman's betrayal of him. Auden's identification of Kallman with Ariel (he identified Kallman with Caliban as well) contributes to a note of plangency throughout Prospero's speech. Finally, Prospero is also conceived in the image of Shakespeare's Prospero, about whom Auden was equivocal. There was a part of the temperament of Shakespeare's Prospero that Auden saw in himself and wished to disavow, particularly the artist's coldness, the tendency to treat human beings largely as aesthetic subjects, as he felt he had treated Kallman, but at the same time he too had been grieved that art could not transform people, and he was more affected by Shakespeare's portrayal of Prospero than he may have been aware (see Introduction, xx–xxii, xxxvii).

Auden told Malcolm Cowley that Prospero's speech to Ariel was in "couplets of thirteen and eleven syllables, with the vowels elided (Malcolm Cowley, "Auden's Versification," *Poetry* 65 [1945]: 345).

Page

5 "revelling wishes": Cf. *Tp*, "Our revels now are ended. . . ." (4.1.148–58).

5 "Briefly Milan, then earth": Cf. *Tp*, "And thence retire me to my Milan, where / Every third thought shall be my grave" (5.1.310–11). Prospero's anticipation of death is a significant undercurrent in *Tp*, and Auden intensifies it in *TSTM*.

5 "So at last I can really believe . . . are very much alive": "Consciousness, they say, cannot conceive of its negation, death. / A bird's still carcase agitates the eye / With novel images. A stranger's sudden end / Is the beginning of much lively speculation. / At eighty bereavement has become a familiar experience / But every time some dear flesh disappears / What is real is the arriving grief" (Berg MS). These lines are from the draft of a speech in *FTB* by the poet-Simeon that criticizes the denial of the reality of death in all human consciousness. Prospero conceives of such denial as a fault of art alone, the result of being "under [the] influence" of Ariel. "What is real is the arriving grief" is a summary of Augustine's discussion, one to which Auden often referred, about how he would rather have been deprived of his friend than of his grief (*Confessions* 4.6). The passage is cited in Auden's notes on the *Confessions* at the end of the Berg MS.

5 "a bird's dry carcase": Altered by proofreader to "carcass" on the galleys.

5 "thanks to your service, / The lonely and unhappy are very much alive": "For the death of others only confirms our conviction / Of being very much alive . . . Their own death is an intellectual fiction / Even to the old" (Berg MS).

5 "the sea / Which misuses nothing because it values nothing": An anticipation of Alonso's thoughts on the sea in Chapter II, one of a number of filaments in the poem connecting Prospero and Alonso, who are also in sympathetic resonance in *Tp*.

5 "So kings find it odd . . . in the thoughts of none": An allusion to the isolation of Shakespeare's King Henry V, in disguise among his soldiers, before the Battle of Agincourt (*Henry V*, 4.1).

6 "a gift / In dealing with shadows": "a gift / Of gentleness with shadows" (Buffalo MS).

6 "When I woke ... the popular earth ... a mere one among many": "Our
first adolescent efforts are scarcely more / Than a substitute for the nursery
rocking-horse / On which we rode away from a father's imperfect justice /
A retort to the insult of being only one among many / A revenge on the
Greeks for their grammar, an atonement / For the humiliating perfor-
mance in the gymnasium / And our passionate conviction of genius almost
as [?unreal] / As the apotheosis we have learned to achieve / By the magical
rites of spring in the locked bathroom" (Berg MS). The protest against the
"Greeks," rather than, as in the final text, the "Romans," suggests its source
in Augustine, who complains in *Confessions* (1.13–14) about the labor of
learning Greek. Augustine is probably also the model for Prospero's lines,
"When I woke into my life, a sobbing dwarf / Whom giants served only as
they pleased," which resemble a passage in *Confessions* (1.6) that Auden
paraphrased as follows in his notes on the work at the end of the Berg MS
of *FTB*: "I was angry because elders did not submit to me, because freemen
would not slave for me, and I avenged myself on them by tears." "Popular
earth" means an earth open to all people. The relation of masturbation,
the "magical rites of spring in the locked bathroom," to the poet's "genius"
echoes a more developed treatment of the subject in the depiction of the
Airman's kleptomania in *The Orators*.

6 "and blot out for ever": As printed in the 1944 edition; "out" was omitted
in *CLP* (1968), as well as in subsequent editions, apparently a compositor's
error.

6 "Now Ariel, I am that I am, your late and lonely master": an ironic echo of
God's call to Moses from the burning bush (Exod. 3.14).

6 "Who knows now what magic is;—the power to enchant / That comes from
disillusion": Behind these lines is Simeon's meditation on the Incarnation
in *FTB*, "Because in Him the Flesh is united to the Word without magical
transformation, Imagination is redeemed from promiscuous fornication
with her own images."

6 "most desires end up in stinking ponds": "Those you lead by the nose / Are
those who think they know what they are looking for / Kingdoms of flesh
and human, comfortable visions / Of gardens that time is for ever outside /
You counterfeit their treasure, impatience does the rest. / Straight after you
into the stinking pond they rush" (Buffalo MS). Cf. Ariel leading Caliban,
Stephano, and Trinculo into a "filthy mantled pool" in *Tp*, 4.1.181–84.

6 "For all things / In your company": Auden deleted a comma after "things"
on the galleys.

7 "No one but you ... unobliged to strike": In the Buffalo MS Auden added, "Finally, my chick, have you performed, your revelations / Exactly correspondent to your promise. / ... Who else could have explained for us the dangerous jungle of the heart[?]"

7 *"Could he but once ... What oncer would not fall in love?"*: In a conversation with Alan Ansen, Auden described a person fearful of a more sustained relation than a one night stand as a "oncer," and applied the term, perhaps untruthfully, to himself.

7 *"The Jolly Elder Brother"*: One way in which Auden thought of his later relation to Chester Kallman; another was as a parent.

8 *"our heathen foe, / For Rome will be a goner"*: In the 1940s, Auden interpreted the fall of Rome to the barbarians, to which he refers also in Alonso's speech, as the consequence of the spiritual failure of classical culture, a view he derived from Charles Norris Cochrane, *Christianity and Classical Culture* (Oxford: Clarendon Press, 1940), a book that he reviewed and admired. See *Prose* II, 226–31, and *LS*, 130–31, 377.

8 *"This dragon that's upon her"*: Andromeda chained for the dragon.

8 "To-day I am free ... freedom": Cf. *DM*, note to line 62, in which Auden elaborates Engels's definition of freedom as the consciousness of necessity. Before this line, in the draft, Auden wrote: "Now that my time has come to leave the island, it seems / No time at all since I arrived, my past a wreck, / My future a void ... / That absolute despair which alone can hear / The ... language of the spirits" (Buffalo MS).

8 "Some feverish young rebel ... his handsome envy": "But when I could manage a few elementary tricks / Like turning discoloured walls into faces / Or achieving [?empathy] with hills or a hill-top fire / Lying in headlands or in chalked quarries, / A feverish rebel among amiable flowers, in / Consultation with my interesting envy, / Thy demands were already less. It seemed sufficient / To be very beautiful and very rich" (Buffalo MS).

8 "All by myself I tempted Antonio ... and neither need be sorry": "The betrayal by a lover or a friend would never have occurred / Unless in some way or other we asked for it" (Buffalo MS). Another version reads: "The evil interest is always present of course / But can't enter until the evil one has found / Some means to know the threshold of resistance / The ill-will of others must wait for a sign from ours / Before it can strike effectively." In *Tp* Prospero acknowledges only that he "Awak'd an evil nature" in Antonio (1.2.93).

9 "discouraged by a pupil's curse": Cf. *Tp*, "You taught me language, and my profit on't it / Is, I know how to curse" (1.2.363–64).

9 "have . . . been soundly hunted . . . into their human selves": Cf. *Tp*, 4.1.257 s.d., 263, and 5.1.213.

9 "To all, then, but me, their pardons": Cf. Prospero's resolve in *Tp* that "The rarer action is / In virtue than in vengeance" (5.1.27–28) and his plea for pardon, with a direct reference to the Lord's Prayer, in the Epilogue.

9 "Alonso's heaviness / Is lost": Cf. Prospero's lines to Alonso in *Tp*: "There, sir, stop. / Let us not burthen our remembrance with / A heaviness that's gone" (5.1.198–200).

9 "Will a Miranda . . . over existing at all?": Cf. Prospero's response in *Tp*, " 'Tis new to thee," to Miranda's declaration of a "brave new world" (5.1.183–84).

9 "Probably I over-estimate their difficulties": "I probably over-estimate these difficulties / For natures less indirect than mine" (Buffalo MS).

9 "*that green remote Cockaigne / Where whiskey-rivers run*": Emendation of "Cockagne" in the 1944 edition and all subsequent editions in Auden's lifetime. Auden may have been thinking of Baudelaire's "un vrai pays de Cocagne," which Auden described in terms of one "desperately homesick for a pre-conscious state" (*Prose* II, 313). "Whiskey-rivers" may be a recollection of Jack Cade's proclamation in *2 Henry VI* that in his Utopia "the pissing conduit" will "run nothing but claret wine" (4.6.2–4). Auden was much amused by Cade (see *LS*, 9, 366).

10 "*Of Heirs Apparent . . . formal feasts*": A reference to Prince Hal's visits to taverns in *Henry IV, Parts One and Two*. Auden may be reacting to Kierkegaard's remark in *Sickness Unto Death*, trans. Walter Lowrie (Princeton: Princeton University Press, 1941), 206, "The incarnate God, if man wanted to be a chum of His, would be an apt counterpart to Prince Henry in Shakespeare." In the background of this stanza is Hal's rejection of Falstaff, which Auden considered soulless.

10 "I feel so peculiar": "I feel so queer" (Buffalo MS).

10 "Stacked up all round my life": "Like [a] stack of unanswered letters" (Buffalo MS).

11 "floating nor flying": "floating nor plying" in galleys and 1944 edition, corrected in subsequent editions.

11 "out over seventy thousand fathoms—?": Kierkegaard's metaphor for the religious life. The question mark was added in *Collected Poetry* (1945).

11 "O Ariel, Ariel, / How I shall miss you": Cf. *Tp*, "Why, that's my dainty Ariel! I shall miss thee (5.1.95).

11 *"Sing, Ariel, sing"*: Auden discarded the following version of a second stanza of this song: "How else shall our mortal / Rebellious flesh / Learn a pride in knowing / That its pride goes pop / . . . / And its loveliest numbers / Amount to nothing / O teach us to turn, / Immortal one / The tables in turn, / Escaping defeat / By rebuking it" (Berg MS).

12 *"out / Of the dozing tree"*: In *Tp* Prospero had freed Ariel from "a cloven pine" in which Sycorax, Caliban's mother, had imprisoned him (1.2.274–81, 291–93).

12 *"With a smoother song / Than this rough world"*: Probably a conflation of Kent's "O, let him pass! He hates him / That would upon the rack of this tough world / Stretch him out longer," in *King Lear* (5.3.313–15), and Prospero's adjuration of "this rough magic" in *Tp* (5.1.50). The third quarto of *King Lear*, however, reads directly: "the rack of this rough world," which Auden may have seen in the Variorum edition of the play.

12 *"Unfeeling god"*: Cf. Ariel's declaration to Prospero in *Tp*, "were I human" (5.1.20). In the Buffalo draft of the earlier part of his speech, Prospero says to Ariel, "Since you, gay interest, have neither heart nor sex nor bowels." He also uses the phrase "childlike interest" to describe Ariel.

12 *"The silent passage / Into discomfort"*: In "Music in Shakespeare", Auden wrote of Prospero's resolution that "every third thought shall be my grave" (5.1.311): "The tone is not that of a man who, putting behind him the vanities of mundane music, would meditate like Queen Katharine 'upon that celestial harmony I go to,' but rather of one who longs for a place where silence shall be all" (Appendix, 67). Nevertheless, the statement by Auden's Prospero "I never suspected the way of truth / Was a way of silence" has a humble inflection, for an artist, and his Prospero also speaks with genuine humility about learning "to suffer / Without saying something ironic or funny / On suffering."

CHAPTER II
The Supporting Cast
(Sotto Voce)

Each member of the cast speaks in a verse form appropriate to his or her character, and they are presented from a variety of sometimes conflicting perspectives (see Introduction, xxii). In a 1932 review of Philip Henderson's edition of John Skelton (*The Complete Works of W. H. Auden: Prose*, Vol. I, ed.

Edward Mendelson [Princeton: Princeton University Press, 1996], 10), Auden had praised Skelton for "the use of different kinds of verse for different characters in *Magnificence*" and contrasted it to the similarity of emotional climaxes in Shakespeare's blank verse. Auden reviewed Skelton while he was writing *The Orators*, which also uses a great variety of poetic forms and meters. Auden added the stage direction (*Sotto Voce*) on the galleys.

In describing Chapter II in a letter to Christopher Isherwood, April 1944 (Huntington Library), Auden said:

> They are again on the sea, (ie living existentially) but they have looked in the mirror. This section consists of their reflections about their reflections Prospero has made each of them see, ie it tries to combine both what they are (as revealed by the artist) and how they riposte to this illumination (the effect of art on people). They may be classified thus:
>
> Antonio—Iago: The man made demonic by art[,] a failure because he cannot forgive forgiveness
>
> Sebastian: The man redeemed by art as failure
>
> Alonso—Henry IV: The abnegation of the via activa (as Prospero abnegates the via contempliva) the one who knows good through evil
>
> Gonzalo—Polonius: The man who makes goodness easy by blinding himself to evil (flight from unconscious resentment into bufferdom)
>
> Ferdinand—Prince Hal, Mr. W.H.: The Male (He for God only)
>
> Miranda: The Female (She for God in him)
>
> Adrian and Francisco: flight from anxiety into chic
>
> Sailors: flight from anxiety into passivity to circumstance
>
> Stephano—Falstaff: flight from anxiety into unconsciousness (body)
>
> Trinculo—Jaques: flight from anxiety into wit (mind).

Most of these descriptions are drawn from lists Auden wrote in the middle of his Buffalo draft, while he was still composing the poem. On the flyleaf of the Buffalo MS, probably before he began working on *TSTM*, Auden wrote the following slightly different and more extensive list of associations among Shakespearean characters: "Prospero—Hamlet / Antonio—Iago / Alonso—Henry IV / Sebastian—Roderigo / Gonzalo—Polonius— [?Antigonus] / Adrian & Francisco—Rosencrantz & Guildenstern / Stephano—Pistol—Bottom / Trinculo—Shallow / Ferdinand—Mr. W. H.—Henry V / Ariel—Puck—Lear's Fool / Caliban—Falstaff."

ANTONIO

Antonio speaks in Dante's *terza rima*. In part because he reflects Auden's inter-
est in Iago as much as in *Tp*'s Antonio, he is more fully Prospero's imaginative
and conscious antagonist than Shakespeare's Antonio is. Like Iago, Auden's
Antonio can perceive, if not entirely understand, good as well as evil. Iago,
for example, sees and envies the beauty of Othello and Desdemona's love:
"O, you are well tun'd now! / But I'll set down the pegs that make this music, /
As honest as I am" (2.1.201–3); and he says that Cassio "hath a daily beauty
in his life / That makes me ugly" (5.1.19–20). Auden's Antonio similarly per-
ceives, and wishes to degrade, the goodness of the characters to whose
speeches he provides a coda, and he can talk knowingly of "the green oc-
cluded pasture" one enters "as a child" that his own existence denies to Pros-
pero. Auden appears to have taken a more circumscribed view of an evil na-
ture later in his life. He wrote in *ACW* that "Good can imagine Evil, but Evil
cannot imagine Good" (201).

In the Buffalo draft, immediately before Antonio's speech, there is a de-
scription of the characters that may represent only his point of view: "Hand-
some you[ths] / Torpid barflies / ~~Honest~~ Withered age / Courtiers / Doting
fathers / Homesick sailors / Nervous envy / Ill-fed clown[s] / ~~Sweet young
things~~ Little girls," corresponding respectively to Ferdinand, Stephano, Gon-
zalo, Adrian and Francisco, Alonso, Master and Boatswain, Sebastian, Trin-
culo, and Miranda.

Page
13 "As all the pigs have turned back into men": An ironic equation of Pros-
pero with Homer's Circe.
13 "the sky is auspicious and the sea / Calm": Cf. *Tp*, "calm seas, auspicious
gales" (5.1.314).
13 "And kissing of course": Proofreader added a comma after "kissing" on
the galleys.
13 "Brother Prospero": "Brother Importance" (Buffalo MS).
13 "What a lot a little music can do ... believe what you say": "One has to
hand it [to] you, / The whole effect is charming: it's wonderful / Really,
how much you have managed to do / To incomplete objects with a little /
Music and simple conjuring. So they / Did want to better themselves after
all. / All over the ship ~~now~~, I hear them pray / As ~~your~~ loyal subjects, ~~to
know their place~~ to be grateful enough, / Trying so hard to believe what

you say. / ~~About life as a dream in search of grace,~~ / ~~And to understand what you mean by the real~~" (Buffalo MS). Cf. "What a Little Moonlight Can Do" from the film *Roadhouse Nights*.

14 "while I stand outside / Your circle, the will to charm is still there": Cf. Prologue to John Dryden and William Davenant's adaptation of *Tp* (1670): "*But* Shakespear's *Magick could not copy'd be, / Within that Circle none durst walk but he.*"

14 "our melancholy mentor . . . the adult in his pride": "You shall remain the grown up, the sage mentor / A man with all man's power, not man's peace" (Buffalo MS).

14 "at the centre / Time turns on": "the centre / Of the ~~great~~ perfected wheel of the forgiven" (Buffalo MS).

14 "The green occluded pasture as a child": "never enter / A little child into the joy of heaven" (Buffalo MS). The published text recollects one of Auden's favorite lines in Baudelaire, from *Moesta et Errabunda*, "Le vert paradis des amours enfantines."

14 "*Your all is partial*": Not a "true *Gestalt*," such as Auden described in *DM*, lines 56–75.

14 "*Your need to love shall never know / Me: I am I, Antonio / By choice myself alone*": A parody of Richard III's declaration in *3 Henry VI*, after the murder of Henry VI, "I have no brother, I am like no brother; / And this word 'love,' which greybeards call divine, / Be resident in men like one another / And not in me! I am myself alone" (5.6.80–83).

FERDINAND

Auden sent a copy of "Ferdinand's Song" to Elizabeth Mayer in a letter dated 9 January 1943 (Berg Collection), with only one significant variant, recorded below. The tone of the mixture of sex and mysticism in the sonnet is difficult to gauge. There is clearly precedent in English poetry for combining religious and erotic imagery, but the tone of Ferdinand's description of "fucking in completely abstract words" (see Introduction, xxiii) is quite different from comparable verse in Donne, for example, and different as well from Auden's own private Christmas letter to Kallman. In a talk at the University of Virginia in 1948 Auden remarked that "art can't deal at all" with either the sexual act or the beatific vision, "experiences where consciousness of what one is doing destroys the pattern that Nature has given to the action" (*Prose* II, 493). See also *Prose* II, 321. In the Buffalo draft, Auden in one list associates Ferdinand with "member," in another with "pecker."

Page

14 "Flesh, fair, unique, and you": Cf. "Dear flesh, dear mind, dear spirit, O
   dear love" in "Canzone."

14 "enrich them so": "enrich them, O" (letter to Elizabeth Mayer, 9 January
   1943, Berg Collection).

14 "Inherit me, my cause": Cf. the discovery of the *I* in the *Thou* in Martin
   Buber's *I and Thou* (1937), a work that interested Auden (see *LS*, 46, 179).

15 "no other promise than touch": "no other promise ~~but~~ than touch" (letter
   to Elizabeth Mayer, 9 January 1943).

15 "The Right Required Time, The Real Right Place, O Light": "Ready re-
   quired time, the good place, the great light" (Buffalo MS). Auden conflates
   Henry James's "The Real Right Thing" with "The Great Good Place," a story
   he interpreted as a religious parable. Cf. "At the Grave of Henry James":
   "To be lame and blind yet burning for the Great Good Place, / To be radi-
   cally corrupt yet mournfully attracted / By the Real Distinguished Thing."

STEPHANO

Auden described the subject of Stephano's ballade in the Buffalo draft as
"mind and body." For analogies with Auden's conception of Falstaff, see his
lecture as well as his essay on *Henry IV, Parts One and Two* (*LS*, 110–12, and
DH, 195–97), in which he speaks of the fat man's "pregnancy" as a solipsistic
equivalent of the creative deed as well as an expression of the wish to return
to the state of innocence that existed before sex.

Page

15 "Between the bottle and the loo": The quotation marks around *loo* in the
   galleys and in all subsequent editions seem clearly to be an editorial intru-
   sion that was prompted by the assumption that American readers might not
   recognize the word. The word is not in quotation marks in Auden's draft
   of Stephano's speech in the Buffalo MS.

16 "Exhausted glasses wonder who": "De jure or de facto, who" (Buffalo
   MS).

GONZALO

In a lecture on *Tp* in the fall of 1941 at the University of Michigan, Auden said
that Gonzalo is "a re-handling of Polonius," but that "Shakespeare now finds
something in the Gonzalo/Polonius type to respect." The character is "now
seen by Shakespeare as essentially good. . . . For the purposes of normal human

life, the gentle, honest soul is best" (Donald Pearce, in *W. H. Auden: The Far Interior*, ed. Alan Bold [Totowa, NJ: Barnes and Noble; London: Vision, 1985], 151–52). Auden's view of Gonzalo and of the association with Polonius is more complicated in *TSTM*, where he is seen, as Auden wrote both in the draft and to Isherwood, as a man who fails to acknowledge the existence of evil. In his New School lecture on the play (*LS*, 297–98, 302), Auden called Gonzalo a "good but stupid character" and disparaged his familiar lines in *Tp* on the ideal commonwealth (2.1.143–68) as "comic and rather dull." He also argued that because Gonzalo "sees Utopia in an ideal future," he is at the end of the play "unrelated to the present." In the draft of *TSTM*, Caliban remarks that "Gonzalo talked / His garden forward fifteen hundred years," but in the final text Gonzalo ends his speech securely in the present, and penitently. Auden modeled Gonzalo's blessing at the end on one of Rilke's *Sonnets to Orpheus* (see note below), but it is paralleled in Gonzalo's benediction in *Tp* as well (5.1.205–13).

Page

16 "Sea and silence": "An ocean calm as our resolve / To remember" (Buffalo MS).

16 "that island where / All our loves were altered": "That island of illusion where / ~~We~~ all came to our senses" (Buffalo MS).

16 "My prediction came to pass": "My ~~conjectures~~ predictions came to pass" (Buffalo MS). Cf. *Tp*, 5.1.205–13.

16 "Words I uttered long ago / Whose glad meaning I betrayed": The consolations Gonzalo offered the King and others in *Tp*, beginning on the apparently sinking ship in the opening scene (1.1.31–33, 49–51) and continuing with his resolute good cheer after they land on the island, including his vision of the ideal commonwealth (2.1.143–68).

17 "I whose interference broke / The gallop into jog-trot prose": "broke / The subtle rhythm into prose" (Buffalo MS). Auden also wrote in the Buffalo draft: "Absence of / Bona fida evidence / Is not the reason to reject / ~~Belief~~ The claim of the infinite."

17 "All have seen the Commonwealth": Cf. *Tp*, 2.1.143–68.

17 "There is nothing to forgive": "Now whichever way I look / There is nothing to forgive / There is everything to bless" (Buffalo MS).

18 "Comfort ambient troubles like / Some ruined tower": The Buffalo draft has "ambient threat of circumstance," and before "Some ruined tower" the lines, "As improbable as the stare / Of rocking horse and teddy bear / By whom the child is comforted." A variant, "The child learns courage from

the stare / Of rocking horse and teddy bear," appears in the draft of Alonso's speech; and a "nursery rocking-horse" alone appears in the draft of Prospero's speech.

18 "Even rusting flesh. . . .": Before these concluding lines, one version in the Buffalo draft reads: "Who is not offended if / Even the mere ~~unfaithful~~ carrier / Whose here and now is close by / The always and already there / As locus for its prophecy / ~~Is found~~ Can be guilty of despair." Another version reads, "Who is less demanded of / Than of him whose here and now / The always and already there / Singles out and asks to be / A locus for its prophecy."

18 "To the lonely—'Here I am', / To the anxious—'All is well' ": Cf. Rilke, *Sonnets to Orpheus*, Second Part, no. 29, trans. M. D. Herter Norton (New York: W. W. Norton, 1942): "And if the earthly has forgotten you, / Say to the still earth: I flow. / To the rapid water speak: I am." Auden also drew upon Rilke's sonnet in speaking of the consolation of art in *DM*, lines 121–26. See also *Tp* (5.1.205–13).

ADRIAN *AND* FRANCISCO

In a letter to Chester Kallman, probably 5 January 1943 (private collection), Auden included the following, far longer, version of Adrian and Francisco's camp couplet:

Adrian The lovely lawns are swarming
   With people no one knows,
  And up the marble staircase run
  A hundred maladjusted girls
   In sensible black hose,
  For milk and fifteen minutes fun
  Between Creative Leatherwork
   And Hygiene of the Nose

Francisco Cupid no longer swishes
   Venus no more behaves,
  Committees take the earth in hand
  To give the hills a thorough scrub
   And sterilize the waves;
  The chief has died of horror, and
  The war-horse and the battle-axe
   Have swept into their graves.

> *Chorus*   Well. Well. Well.
>
> The Old World pooped at the party;
> As the last waltz stopped, she whooped and flopped—
> "Small towns, my dear, are HELL."
> Lay her out in her black silk pajamas,
> Let down your hair and cry:
> *Good little sunbeams must learn to fly,*
> *But it's madly ungay when the goldfish die.*
> *Well. Well. Well.*

This version was reprinted in 1995 in *As I Walked Out One Evening*. According to Ansen, Auden heard the phrase "madly ungay" at a lunch party in the south of France in reference to conditions in Spain at the time of the civil war. He used it to describe one of his classes at Swarthmore in a letter to James Stern, 30 July 1942 (Berg Collection).

ALONSO

Shakespeare's Alonso is marked by love for his son as well as penitence. "It did bass my trespass," he says in *Tp* after seeing Ariel's apparition, "Therefore my son i' th' ooze is bedded; and / I'll seek him deeper than e'er plummet sounded / And with him there lie mudded" (3.3.100–102). The sounding plummet is also associated with the renunciation of art by Prospero, who vows that "deeper than did ever plummet sound / I'll drown my book" (5.1.56–57). Auden may have responded to this association in *Tp* as well as to Alonso's grief itself. He may also have been drawn to Alonso because Alonso's guilt and sorrow over the loss of his son touched upon his own anguish over the loss of Chester Kallman's love.

Auden first published Alonso's speech, a letter intended to be opened by Ferdinand after his death, in *Partisan Review* in October 1943, and he appears to have worked on it more than on any other in Chapter II. There are numerous pages at the beginning of the speech in the Buffalo draft that he discarded, containing false starts as well as material he later used but had not yet crystallized. These draft pages begin with Alonso, not unlike Prospero, contemplating his old age: "Old people should sit by themselves at any time / But ~~especially~~ on sea voyages ~~especially~~ they should be careful / Not to get in anyone's way, not to . . . bother the crew / Who have enough ~~worries~~ to worry about as it is. . . . / Content to ~~watch~~ see the sailors going . . . about their

business / Content to ~~look~~ watch the sun ~~setting~~ sinking calmly into the sea."
He also reflects upon the society of the sailors on the ship, each doing his duty,
together forming a whole, "A ship is like / A city. It is like my own Naples"; and
he says, "With the threat of the sea on one side / And the threat of the desert
on the other, the structures / Of human existence are naturally rather precari-
ous." Contemplating the sea itself, he says: "And when I look at the sea . . . /
A waste of waters, I think of a desert / Space without form, time without
direction / Its existence, even on a calm day, ~~hostile to human life~~ . . . I think
of myself, Alonso, and of those I love / My son Ferdinand, Prospero, freed at
last / Miranda, my daughter in law, and the rest of us, / ~~All of us always in~~
~~danger: I think of death.~~"

A few lines later, Auden inserts a list of distinctions between the sea and the
desert, many drawn from the Swarthmore chart, which was probably com-
posed at the same time, and many of which find their way in various forms
into the published text. The items include: "vagueness and triviality . . . poten-
tiality and necessity . . . agitation without purpose and rest without achieve-
ment . . . essence without form and form without essence . . . sea life city
desert death . . . blind superstition to open despair . . . idiocy to madness . . .
self-sufficiency to self-destruction . . . ignorance of good to certainty of
evil . . . non-becoming to non-being . . . mutual irresponsibility and individual
isolation."

Following the list are several pages in which Alonso contrasts the sea and
the desert: "The first thought that strikes one about the sea," he says in one
version, "Is that it is a freezing abyss which covers everything over / Hiding it
way ~~deep~~ down in a soft darkness. / And the first thought that strikes one
about the desert / Is that it is a scorching surface which reveals everything /
Showing it up in a hard light. / ~~The sea~~ One gives nothing away, the ~~desert~~
other cannot keep a secret / Both are dreadful in their own way; our fear of
the sea / Is our terror of the unknown; our fear of the desert / Is our terror
of ~~exposure~~ others; being exposed ourselves." In a number of subsequent
pages, Alonso examines the idea of the city: "But between the sea and the
desert, ~~for us~~ in our case at any rate / Lies ~~a place for building the city~~ the
little space for life in which to build a city / Where our freedom is a conscious-
ness of our necessity / Or, if you prefer, our necessity is a consciousness of
our freedom." He speculates on the city's growth and progress: "Cooking be-
comes a serious art . . . / The standard of wit is extraordinarily high / All
slaves have been manumitted . . . / Public opinion frowns on drunkenness

and dueling / And there is an excellent . . . sewage disposal system . . . / There are well endowed professorial chairs for the study / Of Truth, Beauty, Goodness, and even ~~the~~ garbagemen / Are ~~learning to~~ taking an intelligent interest in ~~these subjects~~ public affairs." "The sea and the desert lie low," he concludes, "As if they have been taught their place."

But "nothing fails like success," he continues, and in the last of the pages that Auden discarded, Alonso thinks again of the dangers of the sea and the desert, and of the eventual "destruction of the city": "There have always been ~~people~~ some who could not stand city life / There have always been outlaws and exiles but [?until] lately / They were the weak who could not control themselves / Or the selfish who had to be sent away / It is only lately that people have ~~started leaving~~ deliberately chosen to leave / That is the first warning ~~sign~~." At this point in the draft, Auden finds the focus with which the published version begins, as Alonso's thoughts about the sea and desert join with his love of Ferdinand to become the means of expressing his hope for Ferdinand's achievement of "civil order and importance" in his rule as a prince.

Page

19 "keep in mind": "Remember in your time of glory / That the desert and the sea / Are ~~always~~ both present in the kingdom" (Buffalo MS).

19 "The sunburnt superficial kingdom / Where a king is an object": "Remember the glittering mountains to whom / A king is a dark object / When the guests have gone and at last you have led / Your young queen to her enormous bed / Bless her for her perfection but hear / The siren in the ~~darkness~~ blackness . . . / Do not forget as her whiteness lies / Warm in your grateful arms that should anything / Happen to your love, these images / Of hunger and thirst are only too willing / And able to take your place" (Buffalo MS).

20 "The Way of Justice is a tightrope": In 1942, in "Many Happy Returns," Auden wrote to seven-year-old John Rettger, that "Tao is a tightrope," and that to keep his balance he must manage to combine "Intellectual talents / With a sensual gusto / The Socratic Doubt with / The Socratic Sign." "Tao" is a reference to *Tao Tĕ Ching*, the Chinese Quietist writer Lao Tse's treatise on the harmonious conduct of life, "the Way," a mystical philosophy with occasional affinities to Chinese Dualist thought that interested Auden at the time. Auden was introduced to Taoism by his reading of Arthur Waley, *The Way and Its Power* (Boston: Houghton Mifflin, 1935).

20 "The efreet": A variant of "afreet," a powerful evil spirit in Islamic mythology.

20 "Ecbatana": A city of ancient Medea, captured by Cyrus the Great in 549 B.C. and later plundered repeatedly.

21 "From loose craving to sharp aversion": "Between encroachment and aversion" (Buffalo MS).

21 "Island in the sea . . . delivered from mistrust": "Island of vision where flesh and mind / Are made whole again and just" (Buffalo MS).

22 "the solemn / Music . . . the statue move": The reconciliation scene in *The Winter's Tale* (5.3) in which Hermione's statue comes to life. "Solemn music" recollects the music—in *Pericles* specifically the music of the spheres—that marks the resolutions of all of Shakespeare's last plays. Prospero refers to "A solemn air" at the end of *Tp* (5.1.58). Caliban, in his speech in *TSTM*, refers to "that music which explains and pardons all" (40).

MASTER *AND* BOATSWAIN

The elegiac song of the Master and Boatswain, who are labeled "Homesick sailors" in the Buffalo draft, characteristically encompasses the poles of old age and childhood in its portrayal of the consolations of sex. It is an elegant imitation of Stephano's song in *Tp*: "The master, the swabber, the boatswain, and I, / The gunner, and his mate, / Lov'd Mall, Meg, and Marian, and Margery, / But none of us car'd for Kate" (2.2.48–51).

Page

22 "nightingales": Slang term for prostitutes; used by T. S. Eliot in "Sweeney Among the Nightingales."

SEBASTIAN

Auden associated Sebastian, unflatteringly, with Othello's Roderigo at the beginning of the Buffalo MS but commented later in the draft that Sebastian was "redeemed by failure" and that the subject of his sestina was "forgiveness." Shakespeare's Prospero emphasizes that Sebastian's "inward pinches are . . . most strong" (5.1.77); and Sebastian's response to Antonio's temptation in *Tp*, "It is a sleepy language, and thou speak'st / Out of thy sleep" (2.1.211–12), may have prompted Auden's focus on the solipsistic thinking of dreams in Sebastian's speech in the poem (see Introduction, xxvi–xxvii). Auden made comparatively few revisions in the Buffalo draft, but he reversed the order of stanzas 2 and 3 as well as of 5 and 6.

Page

23 "My rioters all disappear . . . it is day": "The bare, and fraying fabric of that dream / Where I, securely wicked, drew my sword / Have ~~suddenly~~ shattered and collapsed. It is clear day" (Buffalo MS).

23 "wicked still": "evil still" (Buffalo MS).

23 "What sadness signalled": "What question signals" (Buffalo MS).

23 "once it is called a proof": "once it has become a proof" (Buffalo MS).

23 "To think his death . . . through the blooming day": "Intent on death, I thought I was alive, / A ~~dark~~ sad cloud ~~walking~~ drifting through a summer day" (Buffalo MS).

23 "The lie of Nothing": "The lie of ~~emptiness~~ evil" (Buffalo MS).

23 "Which cannot be extinguished with some sword: "Which cannot be ~~created with the~~ extinguished by a sword" (Buffalo MS).

24 "Right Here is absolute": "Here" capitalized in *Collected Poetry* (1945).

24 "In dream all sins are easy": "In dream all joys are easy" (Buffalo MS).

24 "*Fights the white bull alone*": Possibly an allusion to the white whale in *Moby Dick* and an association of Antonio with Ahab.

TRINCULO

Auden wrote in the Buffalo draft that the subject of Trinculo's speech, as well as of Stephano's, was "Mind and body," and he clearly counterpoints the two characters. Stephano, who has too much flesh, searches for his mind, while Trinculo, dominated by the coldness of his intellect, tries to find bodily warmth. In the list of the characters in the draft that may be primarily intended to reflect Antonio's view of the characters, Trinculo is also labeled an "Ill-fed clown."

In the Buffalo draft, Auden wrote a different version of Trinculo's speech from the one he printed, and he revised the speech on the galleys as well (see notes below). The opening stanzas in the draft version read:

> The house my father built
>   Far off and long ago
> Had lofty ceilings, I
>   Was little Trinculo.

> The hills looked down upon
>   The valley where I played
> My heart was in my [?breath]
>   And I was not afraid.

> At such and such a place
> In such and such a day
> Came so and so and asked
> My heart to run away.

Page

24 "their fat": Auden revised "the fat" on the galleys.

24 "Quick dreams": Auden revised "My dreams" on the galleys.

25 "These hands": Auden revised "My hands" on the galleys.

25 "My history, my love, / Is but a choice of speech": Auden revised "My hatred and my love / Are limited to speech" on the galleys.

25 "your freezing sky": Auden revised "that freezing sky" on the galleys.

25 "my joke": Auden revised "the joke" on the galleys.

MIRANDA

Miranda's speech immediately follows Ferdinand's in the Buffalo draft. In a description of the characters in the draft that may represent only Antonio's point of view, Miranda is disparagingly labeled "Sweet young thing[s] Little girls," but her villanelle nonetheless uses the fairy-tale idiom of a "little girl" to express a paradisal vision of love and marriage (see Introduction, xxviii–xxix). Like Miranda in *Tp*, she is marked by naïveté and wonder. Caliban's reference in Chapter III to the Muse's possession of "the innocence of a child-like heart to whom all things are pure" describes both Mirandas.

Auden told Malcolm Cowley that Miranda's villanelle, "like the *Lullaby* in his *Christmas Oratorio*, was written in an eleven-syllable line that comes from Ireland: there has to be a caesura after the fifth syllable" (Cowley, "Auden's Versification," 345).

Page

25 "My Dear One is mine as mirrors are lonely": "My dear one is true" (Buffalo MS). The revision suggests the Neoplatonic and Elizabethan conceit of the lover finding her own identity in the image of herself she sees in the eyes of her lover, and may have been partly suggested by Miranda's comment to Ferdinand in *Tp* that she can "no woman's face remember, / Save, from my glass, mine own" (3.1.49–50). In 1942 Auden wrote in *Commonweal* that "in Paradise all mirrors become transparent and so cease to reflect" (*Prose* II, 163).

25 "As the poor and sad are real to the good king": "As the widow's cry is heard by the good king" (Buffalo MS).

25 "high green hill": Possibly suggests Calvary, in the hymn "There Is a Green Hill Far Away." The image may be also, or only, sexual.

25 "the Black Man behind the elder tree": Perhaps an allusion to Othello, who compares himself to "the base Iudean" in the Folio text of *Othello*. In Christian legend, Judas was supposed to have hanged himself from an elder tree.

26 "The Witch . . . Melted into light": Like the Wicked Witch of the West in *The Wizard of Oz* (1939).

26 "as water leaves a spring,": Comma after "spring" added in *CLP* (1968).

26 "At his crossroads": As written in the draft and printed in the 1944 edition; "his" was changed to "the" in *CLP* (1968).

26 "the Ancient": Progressively "the patriarch" and "the Grandfather" in the Buffalo MS.

26 "He kissed me awake": Cf. "Ich küsste Sie wach" in Siegfried's aria in Richard Wagner's *Götterdämmerung*, 3.1.

26 "linked as children in a circle dancing": Cf. *LS*, 151, where Auden refers to a similar image in Lewis Carroll's description of the dance of Tweedledum and Tweedledee in *Through the Looking Glass*. See Introduction, 29.

26 "*The Only One, Creation's O / Dances for Death alone*": "*The Only One, the Royal O / Dances all day alone*" (galleys). Auden's revision on the galleys opposes Miranda's dance in Paradise, the circle of agape, to the Dance of Death. Theodore Spencer apparently prompted the change from "Royal O" to "Creation's O" (see letter to Spencer, 25 February 1944, Harvard University Archives).

CHAPTER III
Caliban

A bravura riposte to what Auden considered Shakespeare's Manichaean interpretation of Caliban in *Tp*, Caliban's speech represents Auden's attempt to capture in a narrative the aesthetic and moral disturbance that Caliban causes in the stage action of *Tp*, and it is a condensation of all the antinomies and crosscurrents of the poem (see Introduction, xxix–xxxii). At once a personification of Nature, specifically the phallus, and a spokesman of art, Caliban talks wittily in Jamesian prose about the inescapable disjunctions between life and art as well as about the "essential emphatic gulf" that lies between "the real Word which is our only *raison d' être*" and both art and life. Auden had precedents for his preoccupation with Caliban in earlier adaptations of *Tp*, notably Robert Browning's *Caliban on Setebos* and Ernest Renan's *Caliban* (see *LS*, 297, 301).

Auden described the "various steps" of Caliban's "address" in a letter to Christopher Isherwood, April 1944 (Huntington Library) as: "1) Echo of Audience. art versus life from the spectator's point of view [27–35]. 2) Address to budding artist (art versus life from the artist's point of view) [35–41]. 3) The flight from God into Nature as immediacy [and] the flight from God into Spirit as possibility Life from the religious point of view [41–44 and 44–46, respectively]. 4) The flight from God into self-reflection. Art from the religious point of view [46–49]. 5) The grand opera as provincial co. and conclusion. Reconciliation of art and life in the religious [49–53]."

Caliban's speech was the section of the poem that Auden found the most difficult to write, but of which he was eventually most proud. He wrote in a letter to Theodore Spencer, ?24 March 1944 (Harvard University Archives), "From May to October [1943], I was completely stuck with Chap III. I knew what I wanted to say, I had the images, but every treatment went awry, until I got the James idea; it seemed blindingly 'right', and bar outside distractions the writing went without a hitch." Auden published the entire speech in his collection of his poetry published by Penguin (1957) and Modern Library (1958). Though there is no extended draft of the published text of the speech, the Buffalo MS has a number of false starts that Auden discarded, but which contain material that he later used. Possibly the first of these is a song by Ariel, "Kiss me Caliban, curse no more," one version of which reads: "The local voice, the visible creation / Greets us again with its grand old calm. / Its wonder and width, the working charm / The sounded note is the restored relation. / Kiss me Caliban, curse no more, / The tears that made trouble between us are gone, / Elsewhere over water in wistful eyes." Another version reads: "Kiss me, Caliban, curse no more, / The hopes that needed our alienation, / The tears that made trouble between us are gone / Elsewhere over water. The wave effaces / Their pledges of purpose from the pliant sand / And the cell is empty where their sadness was" (Buffalo MS).

In the next of the abandoned drafts, Caliban steps forward in front of the curtain at the end of a performance of Shakespeare's play and says, in irregular discursive verse: "Ladies and gentlemen, please keep your seats / An unidentified plane is reported / Approaching the city. I expect only a false alarm. / But naturally we cannot afford / To take any chances. So all our lights are out / And we must sit in the dark. I can guess / What you are all thinking; How odd this feels; to be sitting / In a theatre when the final curtain has fallen, / On a dream that ended ~~most~~ agreeably with wedding bells, / Substantial rewards for the good, and for the bad / Nothing worse than a ~~laugh~~ ducking. . . . / Yet unable to leave and get down / To serious business, by which you mean, the play / Where each of you, including the ladies, / Is cast, you believe, as Prospero, the duke / In charge of the arrangements and the others, / Their disinterested judge, the benevolent / Rector of their chaos." Though Auden discarded these lines, and appears to have wished to exclude explicit allusions to World War II in the poem, the unidentified plane approaching the city and the theater suggests the real context of the war in his mind throughout *TSTM*.

A few lines later, Caliban introduces himself by saying to the audience, "were I to address you / As Trinculo, Miranda, Alphonso, Bosun / Or any ~~other~~ of the names that really fit you, / You would think I meant someone else, your wife perhaps / Or your friend, but certainly not you. Besides / If I call you Prospero, you will recognize / At once who I am. For who can dare / To continue speaking when the play is over/ ~~Lines that are not set down~~ / Interrupting real life with lines that belong / Neither here nor there, but Caliban that savage / the deformed slave, that thing of darkness / Whom, to be Prospero, you must acknowledge as your own."

In another draft of Chapter III, partially in prose and partially in verse, Auden wrote, "There is one problem . . . that any world we know is already a possible world in which we cannot sit side by side unless They are sitting opposite, nor form a circle unless we are turning our backs on Them. Why or how this catastrophe occurred, by which the real world became a possible world, neither you nor I can say. If we adopt myth, if we say that here is a devil— Caliban Setebos who in some unimaginably distant past time bewitched the real world (that drew AB—CD, he turned all the dots in blue, red and yellow) and in whose power it has lain ever since, that is not an explanation, but only a way—perhaps the best way—of stating the fact. The task, both of us agree on that, is to break the spell of Setebos." In exploring the nature of this spell and how it can be broken, Auden drew diagrams of circles with quadrants, wrote equations, and listed the compositions of different colors. Parts of this draft were woven into the published text of Caliban's speech, particularly the description of the "Heaven of the Really General Case" to which Ariel leads his followers, "an allegorical landscape to which mathematical measurement and phenomenological analysis have no relevance" (47). The argument of this draft is often opaque.

In the last of the drafts of Chapter III, Auden wrote a brief passage describing the North Pennine mining landscape of his youth, prefaced by a list of its characteristic features, including an engine with a huge flywheel, a tramway, vats, a stone circle, a Museum, saltmarshes, dunes, the sighting of a whale, hawthorn, bramble. Auden said in "Letter to Lord Byron" (1937): "Tramlines and slagheaps, pieces of machinery, / That was, and still is, my ideal scenery." This scenery appears in the final text of the poem in Caliban's portrayal of the Edenic childhood landscape to which "the general popular type, the major flock" wish to be returned (41). Auden followed the description of northern England in the draft with considerably longer passages depicting a stark, moonlit landscape of lava fields and extinct volcanoes reminiscent of Iceland. Details of these passages also appear in the published text, in Caliban's portrayal of the barren landscape of the "downright state itself" of "the ultimately liberal condition" (45) to which his followers are finally led.

Page

27 *"the indulgence for which in his epilogue your personified type of the creative . . . pleaded"*: Cf. Prospero's Epilogue in *Tp*: "As you from crimes would pardon'd be, / Let your indulgence set me free."

27 *"Our native Muse . . . mixed perfect brew"*: Caliban compares the panoramic freedom of Elizabethan drama to the strictness of the focused drama of ancient Greece ("Grecian aunt") and neoclassical France ("Gallic sister"). As he goes on to explain, however, even an English audience must draw the line at the introduction of a character as aesthetically disruptive as himself. Cf. *Prose* II, 165–66, 366–69; *LS*, 179,195–96; *DH*, 172–76, where Auden elaborates the moral consequences of the differences between Elizabethan and Greek drama.

27 *"just tout le monde"*: Proofreader added emphasis to *"tout le monde"* on the galleys.

28 *"the bohemian standardless abyss,"*: Comma after *"abyss"* added in *CLP* (1968).

28 *"the real, the only test"*: Comma after *"only"* added in *CLP* (1968).

29 *"indeed yes, O there is"*: Proofreader corrected *"indeed yes othere is"* on the galleys, appropriately capitalizing the "O."

29 *"her Awful Enemy . . . 'that envious witch'"*: Sycorax, Caliban's mother in *Tp*. In the play Prospero describes her as a "foul," not an "envious," witch (1.2.258).

29 *"lying in wait for its vision of private love or public justice . . . fishlike odour or bruit insolite snatching . . . to the here and now"*: "Experience should have

taught you, / What even my dumb presence ~~does to language~~ can do, that, when / Miranda and Ferdinand have spoken themselves to giants / Swooning in Egypt, or Gonzalo talked / His garden forward fifteen hundred years, / One fish-like smell from me, one ~~slight~~ low / Insolent sound can wrench ~~them from their language~~ these travellers back / Tongue-tied and blushing to the here and now. / And then to allow me language. You were mad / ~~C~~an you have [?hoped] I should use your words / As you do, as a magic to ~~remove~~ favour what is[,] / To throw away three quarters of itself" (Buffalo MS). "Giants / Swooning in Egypt" is a reference to Shakespeare's Antony and Cleopatra (see *LS*, 236–42, and Introduction, xxiv).

29 *"she dreaded, what"*: Comma after *"dreaded"* added in *CLP* (1968).

29 *"spoiling their fun"*: Emphasis to "their" was added by Auden on the galleys, but the proofreader and compositor ignored his change.

29 *"His making . . . a pass at her virgin self"*: An allusion to Caliban's attempt to rape Miranda in *Tp* and a passing identification of Miranda with "our native Muse."

30 *"conspirator and his victim, the generals of both armies"*: The comma after "victim" is an emendation of a semicolon in the 1944 edition.

31 *"an elegant contrapposto"*: Emphasis was added to *"contrapposto"* by the proofreader on the galleys.

31 *"we are not, we re-iterate"*: Proofreader deleted the hyphen in *"re-iterate"* on the galleys.

31 *"does not, like hers, enjoy an infinitely indicative mood"*: Cf. "a rising of the subjective and subjunctive to ever steeper stormier heights" in the hell to which Ariel leads his followers in Caliban's speech (49); and *DM*, note to line 829: "The poetic mood is never indicative."

31 *"inflected gamut of an alien third, since"*: Comma after "third" added in *CLP* (1968).

31 *"without a . . . Them to turn the back on, there could be no . . . Us to turn the eye to . . . Space is never the whole uninhibited circle but always some segment. . . . For without these prohibitive frontiers we should never know who we were or what we wanted"*: The discussion of the human need for boundaries is derived from the section of the draft of Chapter III in which Auden describes the "spell of Setebos" that has turned the "real world" into a "possible world."

31 *"Space is never"*: 1944 edition printed "space to never"; corrected to "space is never" in *Collected Poetry* (1945). Emendation of "space" to "Space" by Edward Mendelson (*Collected Poems*, 1991) to parallel capitalized "Time" in succeeding passage.

32 *"trespass of any unqualified stranger, not a whit less"*: Comma after "stranger," as in the galleys and 1944 edition.

32 *"seize the post-office"*: Proofreader deleted the hyphen in *"post-office"* on the galleys.

32 *"logic and instinct require that. Of course, We and They"*: As corrected by Auden in *CLP* (1968). Printed as "logic and instinct require that—of course. We and They" in the 1944 edition.

33 *"our devoted pungent expression of"*: Auden revised "our utter devotion to" on the galleys.

33 *"So, too, with Time who, in our auditorium, is not . . . whose court never adjourns"*: Auden revised "So with Time, who, on her stage, in an auditorium, is not" on the galleys. Cf. Kafka's aphorism, quoted in *DM*, note to line 142: "Only our concept of Time makes it possible for us to speak of the Day of Judgment by that name; in reality, it is a summary court in perpetual session."

33 *"conscious that there are others who have not been so fortunate, others who did not succeed in navigating the narrow passage. . . ."*: "The truck missed us by inches / The bomb fell on the next street / The famine chose another country / We negotiated the pelvic passage. We were not eaten by cannibals when we landed. There was food and drink. We rested a little and set off. The bandits left us alone. We did not look important enough. We tripped, we lost the path at times. We arrived at the city" (Buffalo MS). Caliban's stress on the less fortunate mirrors the sense of guilt, which Auden frequently discussed in his letters, over his own privileged situation, including his exclusion from military service in World War II because of his homosexuality. On the galleys, Auden revised, or corrected, "conscious that there were others who have not been so fortunate," changing "were" to "are."

33 *"You . . . have spoken of the conjured spectacle as 'a mirror held up to nature'"*: Cf. Hamlet's address to the players: "the purpose of playing, whose end, both at the first and now, was and is, to hold, as 'twere, the mirror up to nature; to show virtue her own feature, scorn her own image, and the very age and body of the time his form and pressure" (3.2.22–27).

33 *"their mutual reversal of value"*: Auden corrected *"the mutual reversal of value"* on the galleys, probably a typist's or compositor's misreading.

34 *"the absolutely natural, incorrigibly right-handed. . . . He couldn't appear as anything but His distorted parody, a deformed and savage slave"*: Auden corrected "right-minded" on the galleys, probably a typist's or compositor's misreading. Caliban's image cannot be transformed (reversed from right to left)

by reflection in the mirror of art. Caliban is described as "a salvage and deformed slave" in the *dramatis personae* of *Tp*.

34 "*the nude august elated archer of our heaven, the darling single son of Her . . . our great white Queen of Love herself*": Auden revised "august nude archer" on the galleys. Eros and Venus, respectively, are identified with Caliban and his mother Sycorax, the Muse's "Awful Enemy."

35 "*the damage which the poetic would inflict if it ever succeeded in intruding upon the real*": Auden said that "A society constructed to be like a beautiful poem" would be a tyranny, a "nightmare of horror" (*LS*, 84; see also *Prose* II, 348, 349; *DH*, 85).

36 "in the middle of a saltmarsh": Altered by proofreader to "salt marsh" on the galleys. In the draft of *FTB* (Berg MS), Simeon, an aging poet rather than the prophet of the final version, speaks of the awakening of his gift of poetry: "Once when I was fifteen years old, and I walked / At three o'clock on a Sunday afternoon / On a narrow causeway in the middle of a saltmarsh / When I suddenly knew what I was going to be."

36 "observes through the keyhole, He": Auden changed a semicolon after "keyhole" on the galleys to a comma, but his correction was ignored by the compositor.

36 "where the cabinet minister": Auden corrected, or revised, "when the cabinet minister" on the galleys.

37 "relationship between magician and familiar": In the draft of *FTB*, Auden speaks of "the relationship of oneself to one's vocational gift / By the analogy of a marriage," an analogy he frequently discussed in his prose. The relation "between magician and familiar" evokes Prospero's role as a magician in *Tp* as well as his relationship with Ariel.

37 "No perception however *petite*": "*Petite*" italicized by Auden in *CLP* (1968). An allusion to Leibniz's notion of the unconscious perceptions ("*petites perceptions*") that help make up conscious perception ("*apperception*").

37 "for by then your eye has already spotted . . . one appalling laugh": Auden transposed this passage from the Buffalo draft of Alonso's letter to Ferdinand, where it described the powers not of an artist but of a successful prince.

37 "gentle and remedial,": Emendation—comma added after "remedial."

38 "stammer or shout": Auden corrected "stammer a short" on the galleys, probably a a typist's or compositor's misreading.

38 "Striding up to Him in fury": Auden corrected "Standing up to him in fury" on the galleys, probably a typist's or compositor's misreading.

39 "the only subject that you have": The pun on artistic and political "subject" alludes to Caliban's lines in *Tp*, "For I am all the subjects that you have, / Which first was mine own king" (1.2.341–42).

39 "the all too solid flesh you must acknowledge as your own": A conflation of Hamlet's: "O that this too too solid flesh would melt, / Thaw, and resolve itself into a dew!" (1.2.129–30); and Prospero's: "this thing of darkness I / Acknowledge mine" (5.1.275–76).

39 "your dish, how completely": Proofreader changed a comma after "dish" on the galleys to a semicolon; "now" in the 1944 edition corrected to "how" in *Collected Poetry* (1945).

39 "all-forgiving because all-understanding": Hyphens were added in *Collected Poetry* (1945).

39 "the reverent rage of the highest-powered romance": Cf. "The reverent fury of couples on the wedding night," *DM*, note to lines 1649–50.

40 "that music which explains and pardons all": The celestial harmony of the music of the spheres. See also note to the last lines of Alonso's speech (91).

40 "smack into that very same truth": Auden added "very" on the galleys.

40 "Good Right Subject": Like "the Real Right Place" in the final line of Ferdinand's sonnet, an allusion to Henry James's "The Real Right Thing" and "The Great Good Place."

40 "holes in the table cloth": Altered by proofreader to "tablecloth" on the galleys.

41 "the more candid more luxurious world": Proofreader added a comma after "candid" on the galleys.

41 "your charms . . . have cracked and your spirits . . . have ceased to obey": Cf. Prospero, *Tp*, "My charms crack not, my spirits obey" (5.1.2).

41 "the dark thing you could never abide to be with": Cf. Prospero, *Tp*, "But thy vile race, / Though thou didst learn, had that in't which good natures / Could not abide to be with" (1.2.358–60). See also 5.1.275–76.

41 "speak of your neglect of me as your 'exile', of the pains you never took with me as 'all lost'?": Prospero says of Caliban in *Tp*, "on whom my pains, / Humanely taken, all, all lost, quite lost!" (4.1.189–90), but he does not speak of "exile," a word that never appears in the play.

41 "of my getting a tolerably new master and you a tolerably new man": Cf. Caliban's song in *Tp*, " 'Ban, 'Ban, Ca—Caliban / Has a new master. Get a new man" (2.2.188–89).

41 "the girding on of coal-scuttle and poker should transform you into noble Hector": An allusion to Don Armado performing Hector in *Love's Labour's Lost* (5.2).

42 "relation to your present": 1944 edition printed "to you present"; corrected in *Collected Poetry* (1945).

42 "you have now all come to together": Proofreader misconstrued the sense of the phrase and deleted "to" on the galleys.

42 "The Journey of Life": An emendation of "life" in the galleys and first edition. The capital "L" seems intended. When Auden made a taped reading at Yale in 1959, he wrote on the box the titles of the pieces he read, and he twice capitalized the "L" in listing this part of the speech (correspondence from Edward Mendelson).

42 "gorgeous or drab": Auden revised "gorgeous or horrid" on the galleys.

43 "one vast important stretch the nearer Nowhere": Cf. Rainer Maria Rilke, *Duino Elegies*, trans. J. B. Leishman (New York: Norton, 1939), "The Eighth Elegy"—"always world, / and never nowhere without no." Cf. *DM*, lines 1544–46: "the Essential Stone, / 'The Nowhere-without-No' that is / The justice of societies"; and note to line 1545, in which Auden quotes Rilke's text (in German).

43 "jollier more various crowd": Proofreader added a comma after "jollier" on the galleys.

43 "uncomfortable and despotic certainties": Proofreader added a comma after "despotic" on the galleys.

44 "Oh how awfully": Proofreader changed "Oh" to "oh" on the galleys.

44 "lingos": Altered by proofreader to "lingoes" on the galleys.

44 "Marine Biological Station . . . Devil's Bedposts": These references have northern England connotations. Among marine biological stations, Auden probably knew of Millport in the Firth of Clyde, Cullercoats near the mouth of the Tyne, and Robin Hood's Bay near Whitby, all of which have adjacent beaches and conspicuous windows. The Devil's Bedposts may be a reference to The Devil's Arrows, three Bronze Age standing stones close to the Great North Road at Boroughbridge, or possibly The Devil's Bed and Bolster, an antiquity at Rode in Somerset. See Alan Myers and Robert Forsythe, *W. H. Auden: Pennine Poet* (North Pennines Heritage Trust: Nenthead, Cumbria, England, 1999), 44. In the draft Auden also writes of "Oyster Clough," "carved tombs / At Downfell, the magnificent large mirror in the bar at the Moorcock," and "a hydropathic establishment [at] Skinface Trough" (Buffalo MS).

44 "Black currant bushes": "Current" corrected to "currant" in *Collected Poetry* (1945).

45 "waterwheel—; to the north": Proofreader deleted the semicolon on the galleys.

45 "O Cupid, Cupid . . . for our undistress": Emendations—there are no quotation marks in the 1944 edition, as the sense requires, after the second *Cupid*, before *take*, and after *undistress*, at the end of the paragraph.

45 "We're so so tired": Proofreader added a comma after the first "so" on the galleys.

45 "any cathedral town or mill town or harbour or hill side or jungle or other specific Eden": Auden substituted "Eden" for "Americas" on the galleys. He wrote Theodore Spencer, ?24 March 1944 (Harvard University Archives), "Thanks a lot for pointing out 'Americas' which of course is not 'the Newfoundlands' but 'Edens'. The symbolic landscapes here have to be built up from personal childhood experiences or they would sound phoney. E.g. 'sixpence' has an underground relation to sex and penis and it would be quite impossible for me as an immigrant to know the American equivalent. For 'sugarloaf sea', see American Thesaurus of Slang, p. 790" [by Lester V. Berrey, New York: Thomas Crowell, 1942].

45 "hill side": Altered by proofreader to "hillside" on the galleys.

45 "Directly overhead a full moon . . . still and sharp": "Overhead in a night without stars, a full moon ~~blazes~~ of dazzling brilliance emphasizes the absence of any third party. It is a waste without forms, a world without wishes, bearing the stamp of a winter which ~~you can~~ it will never explain. Every object is already there, extraordinary still and sharp. . . . All this vast area has been a scene of prodigious convulsions and violence, but to ask how long ago would be absurd, since what you mean by time began with its ~~petrification~~ total exhaustion. It was never a battleground, only the ~~place~~ occasion of one enormous disappointment. Energy, to which nothing would have been impossible, burst ~~forth from~~ out of the earth and found it was not needed. It spent itself and stopped. . . . Now it is too late" (Buffalo MS).

46 "clinkers": Cooled lava.

46 "Confronted by a straight . . . surrounded by an infinite": Auden revised "her straight" and "her infinite" on the galleys.

46 "my more spiritual colleague?": Emendation—question mark added after "colleague."

46 "sugarloaf sea": A rough sea, with pointed waves, from *American Thesaurus of Slang* (1942).

47 "that Heaven of the Really General Case": A transcendental universe of self-reflection, an unparticularized world without causal necessity to which Ariel leads those, including poets who "gave the caesura its freedom," who wish to escape from the chaos of life and are in "flight from God into Spirit as possibility." "The artist's maxim," Auden wrote in 1939 in *The Prolific and the Devourer,* is that " 'Whoso generalises, is lost' " (*Prose* II, 421).

47 "Life turns into Light:" An echo of Miranda's lines, "The Witch gave a squawk; her venemous body / Melted into light as water leaves a spring."

48 "balloons are available": Proofreader added a comma after "balloons" on the galleys.

48 "There is probably no one": Proofreader changed "There" to "there" on the galleys.

49 "fish-tail burner": A type of gas lamp.

49 "ever steeper stormier heights": Proofreader added a comma after "steeper" on the galleys.

49 "delirious gush of glossolalia": Auden corrected "gusto" to "gush" on the galleys, probably a typist's or compositor's misreading.

49 "this nightmare of public solitude, this everlasting Not Yet, what relief": Auden added "this everlasting Not Yet," on the galleys.

49 "bisson eye and bevel course": Cf. "bisson rheum" (*Hamlet*, 2.2.502), blinding tears. "Bevel course" means at an obtuse angle.

49 "the Black Stone": Lowercase in 1944 edition; capitalized by Auden in *CLP* (1968).

49 "the love nothing, the fear all": Cf. Lady Macduff: "All is the fear, and nothing is the love" (*Macbeth*, 4.2.12).

51 "the smiling interest": The poet's elusive gift, with an allusion to Henry James's fondness for discussions of "the interest" or "the interest itself" in works of art.

51 "the greatest grandest opera rendered by a very provincial touring company indeed": Borrowed, Auden told Alan Ansen, from the writings of Leon Trotsky.

51 "the *Landsknecht*": Mercenary, professional actor. Emended to capital "*L*"; "*landsknecht*" in the galleys and 1944 edition.

51 "orchestra we could scarcely hear, for half": Comma after "hear" added by Auden in *CLP* (1968).

51 "the stud contralto gargling through her maternal grief": Auden revised "the bereaved contralto gargling through her grief" on the galleys.

52 "the unearthly harvesters hysterically entangled in their honest fugato": A
   parodic recollection, probably, of the "country footing" of the "sunburn'd
   siclemen" in the wedding masque for Ferdinand and Miranda in *Tp*
   (4.1.134–38). It is likely, also, that "the huge stuffed bird of happiness" in
   the following paragraph glances at the entire masque, which is presented
   by the saffron-winged Iris and in which Ceres sings fulsomely of "Earth's
   increase, foison plenty, / Barns and garners never empty, / Vines with
   clust'ring bunches growing, / Plants with goodly burthen bowing"
   (4.1.110–14). Auden marked this passage in his copy of Kittredge's edition
   of *The Complete Works of Shakespeare* (see *LS*, xi, 361).

52 "never stood anywhere else,—when"; "never has been,—and our wills";
   "There never was,—it is": Commas and dashes reversed in 1944 edition;
   corrected in *Collected Poetry* (1945).

52 "first time in our lives": Auden revised "first time in our naughty lives" on
   the galleys.

52 "as born actors": Auden revised "with the imbecile vanity of the born actor"
   on the galleys.

52 "Not that we have improved; everything, the massacres": Auden revised
   "have improved; Oh, dear, no; everything, the massacres" on the galleys.

52 "that Wholly Other Life": The *ganz andere*, as Rudolph Otto named the
   holy, a phrase echoed in the theology of Barth, Niebuhr, and Tillich.

52 "it is precisely in its negative image of Judgement that we can positively
   envisage Mercy": A restatement of the traditional Christian belief that
   Mercy does not replace the Law but fulfills it.

52 "the bones": Auden revised "the smelly old bones" on the galleys.

53 "molar pardon": Wolfgang Köhler referred to "the 'macroscopic' or
   'molar' aspect of the physical world" in *The Place of Value in the World of
   Facts*, 169.

53 "its spaces greet us . . . the restored relation": These lines were originally
   part of the draft of the lyric Auden wrote for Ariel, "Kiss me Caliban, curse
   no more" (see note, 95).

POSTSCRIPT

Auden transplanted the verses of the Postscript from the draft of *FTB* (Berg
MS), where they may have originally been written for the voice of Simeon's
poetic gift, before Auden decided to make Simeon a theologian. Their adapta-
tion to the voice of Ariel speaking to Caliban in *TSTM* is inherent in the
original *FTB* draft and suggests the degree to which Auden's interpretations

of Shakespeare's two characters were incipient in his thought. The religious subtext of the Postscript, like that of the Preface, also illustrates how much of a continuum *FTB* and *TSTM* formed in his imagination.

Ariel's plea to Caliban expresses the hope for the reconciliation of flesh and spirit not only in the artist but in all the human beings represented by the Prompter's "I," including Prospero, of whom Caliban and Ariel are allegorical components, as well as Auden himself. Auden added the Prompter's "I" late in the draft, crossing out the line "Should one falter both would die," or a slight variant, that formed the final refrains of all three stanzas. He wrote in *FTB* that "The singular is not Love's enemy; / Love's possibilities of realisation / Require an Otherness that can say *I*."

Page

55 "*(Ariel to Caliban. Echo by the Prompter)*": Added by proofreader on the galleys, evidently working from Auden's instructions.

55 "Weep no more . . . Fleet persistent shadow cast . . . Drab mortality;": "Seek no more, rejoice in me / The unwanted shadow cast / By your lameness, found at last / Helplessly in love with you / Order, energy, and beauty / Fascinated by / Drab stupidity" (Berg MS). The "shadow" is the negative side of personality, everything that one does not want to be, a notion derived from Carl Jung.

55 "For my company . . . if you will cry": "For my honour's sake be lonely / Arrogant and ill / Save me from disloyalty" (Berg MS).

55 "Never hope to say farewell . . . One evaporating sigh / . . . *I*": "Never hope to say farewell / Nor while living plan to part / For the lady of your heart / Or the honourable drum / This was long ago decided / Both of us know why, / Can, alas, foretell / Should our falsehoods be divided / What we should become / I shall sing as you shall sigh / If one falters both would die" (Berg MS).

Printed in the USA
CPSIA information can be obtained
at www.ICGtesting.com
LVHW090442151223
766409LV00002B/338